The Eleven Towns Railway

THE STORY OF THE MANCHESTER AND LEEDS MAIN LINE

JEFFREY WELLS

RAILWAY & CANAL HISTORICAL SOCIETY

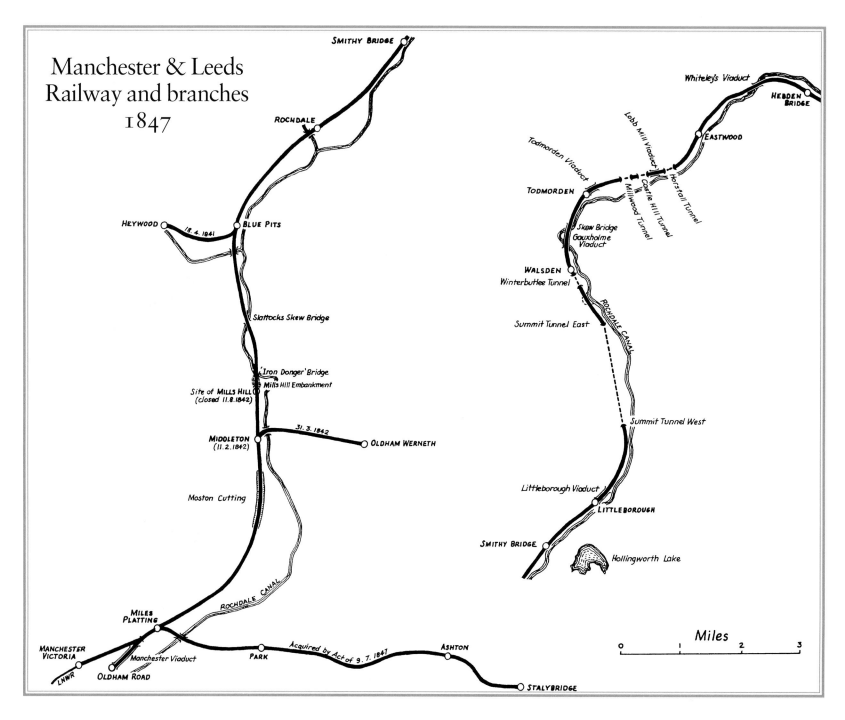

Manchester & Leeds
Railway and branches
1847

SMITHY BRIDGE

Whiteley's Viaduct

HEBDEN BRIDGE

ROCHDALE

EASTWOOD

Lobb Mill Viaduct

Todmorden Viaduct

TODMORDEN

Horsfall Tunnel

Castle Hill Tunnel

Millwood Tunnel

HEYWOOD

18.4.1841

BLUE PITS

Skew Bridge

Gauxholme Viaduct

WALSDEN

Winterbutlee Tunnel

Slattocks Skew Bridge

ROCHDALE CANAL

Summit Tunnel East

'Iron Donger' Bridge

Mills Hill Embankment

Site of MILLS HILL
(closed 11.8.1842)

31.3.1842

MIDDLETON
(11.2.1842)

OLDHAM WERNETH

Summit Tunnel West

Moston Cutting

Littleborough Viaduct

LITTLEBOROUGH

SMITHY BRIDGE

Hollingworth Lake

MILES
PLATTING

ROCHDALE CANAL

MANCHESTER
VICTORIA

Manchester Viaduct

PARK

Acquired by Act of 9.7.1847

ASHTON

LNWR

OLDHAM ROAD

STALYBRIDGE

Miles

0   1   2   3

2

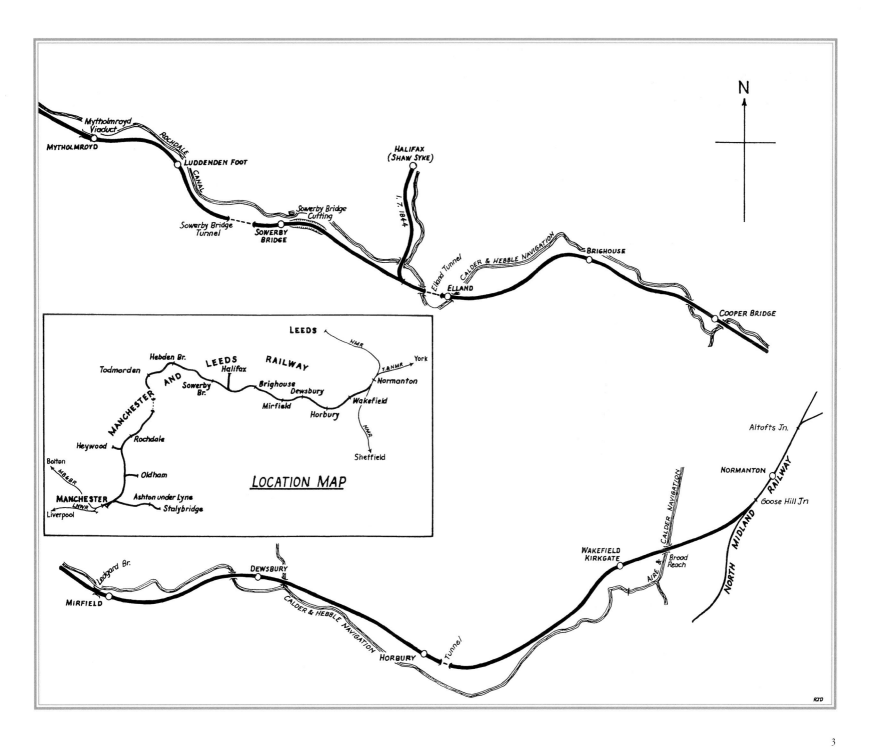

N

MYTHOLMROYD
Mytholmroyd Viaduct
ROCHDALE CANAL
LUDDENDEN FOOT
Sowerby Bridge Tunnel
SOWERBY BRIDGE
Sowerby Bridge Cutting
HALIFAX (SHAW SYKE)
1.7.1844
Elland Tunnel
CALDER & HEBBLE NAVIGATION
ELLAND
BRIGHOUSE
COOPER BRIDGE

LEEDS
NMR
Hebden Br.
Todmorden
LEEDS AND RAILWAY
Halifax
Y.& NMR
York
MANCHESTER
Sowerby Br.
Brighouse
Dewsbury
Normanton
Mirfield
Horbury
Wakefield
Heywood
Rochdale
NMR
Bolton
M.B.& B.R.
Oldham
Sheffield
MANCHESTER
Ashton under Lyne
LNWR
Stalybridge
Liverpool

LOCATION MAP

Altofts Jn.

NORMANTON
Goose Hill Jn
NORTH MIDLAND RAILWAY

Ledgard Br.
DEWSBURY
WAKEFIELD KIRKGATE
CALDER & HEBBLE NAVIGATION
AIRE & CALDER NAVIGATION
Broad Reach
MIRFIELD
HORBURY
Tunnel

RTD

3

TO JEAN

First published in 2000 by the
Railway & Canal Historical
Society

Registered office:
77 Main Street, Cross Hills,
Keighley, West Yorkshire BD20 8PH

Registered charity no.256047

© 2000 Railway & Canal
Historical Society

ISBN 0 901461 21 0

Designed and typeset by
Malcolm Preskett

Printed in England by
Biddles Ltd, Guildford, Surrey

Cover illustrations taken from
engravings by A.F. Tait
front: Brighouse Station – 'One
of the most important stations
on the line'
back: Gauxholme Viaduct
which carried the M&L over the
Rochdale Canal
(NMPFT/Science & Society
Picture Library)

Contents

Introduction

THE sobriquet 'the single thread' for this pioneering railway occurred to me whilst awaiting the arrival of a train at Manchester Victoria station. Having the time to ponder, I scrutinised the tiled map which adorns one of the walls of the concourse, a well-known map which depicts the full extent of the Lancashire & Yorkshire Railway system. The system of this Company has a characteristic east-west (or west-east) alignment, something akin to the shape of a dumb-bell, with a bulbous end occupying each of the counties. The two are united by a single thread of railway which winds its way through the Pennine Hills via natural features of the landscape and by man-made structures, a line of railway which has for over 150 years been the means of conveyance of people, materials and ideas.

The 'single thread' was from the beginning a most singular thread because of its place in the early development of railways in the north of England. It was from this one railway, projected, engineered and operated by the Manchester & Leeds Company, that the better known Lancashire & Yorkshire Railway developed and expanded, its branches and connections with other companies' railways taking place during the last half of the nineteenth century.

The main line, often referred to as the Calder Valley Line, owes its origin to the vision and determination of the early promoters of the Manchester & Leeds Railway. This Company was a striking exemplar of nineteenth-century endeavour, an endeavour moreover, which was confined to a time span of ten years (1837–47). The genesis of the Company 'this great national undertaking', as one sagacious observer referred to it, occurred in 1836, a little over ten years after the abandonment of the inchoate proposal of 1825. Its development took place against a background of social unrest and change in the wake of the Napoleonic Wars, and in the first decade of Queen Victoria's reign. In the years leading up to 1847, the Manchester & Leeds matured into an operation determined on expansion, and this it did with such aplomb and success that it metamorphosed with ease into the Lancashire & Yorkshire Railway by an Act of Parliament – the same railway but with a different name.

To fully appreciate the soul and character of the Manchester & Leeds Railway, it is useful to recall events and incidents which took place during its existence. It is through the eyes and experiences of those who were directly involved in its making, and of those who faithfully recorded what they saw, that the rich kaleidoscope of the Company's main line can be told.

Acknowledgements

IT was not until I set out to write these acknowledgements that I realised the weight of those who deserve recognition. I am indebted to a number of people who provided help with the preparation of this book, and to the staff of several institutions who bore my requests for heavy tomes and information with courtesy and interest.

A photograph is said to save a thousand words. Without such images the book would be a dull exposé of this pioneer railway. This being so, I extend my thanks to David Ibbotson, Jim Peden and Tom Wray, and to my colleagues in the Lancashire & Yorkshire Railway Society for giving me the opportunity of reproducing their respective photographs. Many of the original M&L structures are extant so allowing me to record their presence on camera. These have also been included.

I am grateful to Tom Wray for his initial reading of CHAPTER 7, and to Roger Mellor for the companionship and help on each visit to the Public Record Office. The mammoth task of proof-reading the entire manuscript fell to John Marshall to whom I am most grateful for his meticulous attention to detail and for his valuable advice.

Maps of the M&L route have been redrawn by Richard Dean from my crude tracings, whilst Malcolm Preskett embraced the task of design from a bundle of papers, drawings and photographs. I thank them both for their professionalism and friendly co-operation.

Much of the factual content was obtained from Manchester Central Library. My visits to this venerable place were so frequent that I became almost part of the fittings! Further material was obtained from the John Rylands Library, Manchester, the Greater Manchester County Record Office, Wakefield Public Library, and the Bronte Parsonage Museum, Haworth. It is to all of them that I owe a great deal.

If, after reading this book, the reader knows a little (or more) about 'The Eleven Towns Railway' then my purpose will have been accomplished.

JW 1999

ONE

A Decade of Change
1837–1847

THE seven-year reign of William IV came to an end at 2 a.m., 20 June 1837. In the following year, on the 28 June, the coronation of the 18-year-old Victoria heralded a new era. As Queen, Victoria was to watch over manifold changes affecting the lives of her subjects, her first six years as sovereign embracing a time of severe recession. As one author has put it:

> in 1836 the good harvest and trade boom came to an end, and by 1837 the country was plunged into a prolonged depression lasting until 1842. These six years were the grimmest period in the history of the Nineteenth Century. Industry came to a standstill, unemployment reached hitherto unknown proportions, and with high food prices and inadequate relief the manufacturing population faced hunger and destitution.[1]

Although conditions were to improve in 1843, the daily lives of the mass of ordinary people were of hardship and unremitting toil. It is not surprising that the popular movement known as Chartism flourished between 1837 and 1847, and reached its zenithal influence between 1838 and 1842. This movement, born out of the public disillusionment with the Great Reform Act of 1832, was held together in common pursuit of electoral reform by its mentors Feargus O'Connell and William Lovett. By the late summer of 1842, the year of the Plug Riots, national insurrection was in the air. A general strike involving 500,000 workers was sparked off by the demand for wage reductions in the cotton mills of Ashton

and Stalybridge, quickly spreading to Manchester, the rest of Lancashire, Cheshire and Yorkshire.

It was in this county (Lancashire) that the greatest share of industrial workers were concentrated, where industrial revolution took form and shape, and where in 1842 the most advanced factories stood derelict, their workers idle, victims of a profound economic crisis.[2]

The strike was a passionate cry of the hungry and destitute which spilled over into often violent action, where 'Hordes of rough-looking men in fur caps, carrying clubs and faggots patrolled the squalid unpaved roads around the idle mills; others attempted to hold up the mail and tear up the permanent way on the Manchester–Leeds Railway.'[3] Only by the action of the military was the country saved from total revolution in pursuit of Chartist claims. The strikers, many of whom were women in support of their husbands and fathers, were confronted with armed militia who fired at the rioters when the situation seemed to be getting out of hand. In great distress, stalked by hunger and feeling the harassment and intimidation of various government measures, the strikers backed down and returned to work. After seven weeks the general 'turn-out' ended, the mills and factories reopened, and the pitiless regime started once again – and without a penny being advanced as an increase of wages. Chartism, which had been much a part of the general strike, a class struggle for the rights of man, lingered on until 1858 when the last vestiges of the movement no longer had any relevance.

Working conditions for the mass of people differed according to the kind of employment undertaken. Increasingly

1. J.F.C. Harrison, *Early Victorian Britain*, p.34.

2. M. Jenkins, *The General Strike of 1842*, p.42.

3. Sir Arthur Bryant, *A History of Britain and the English People*, Vol.3, p.89.

after 1815, the agricultural worker, denied his own land, had been forced to work for the landowners, or escape the countryside and head for the urban areas. Hitherto, he had maintained his small holding and supplemented his meals and income by indulging in a spot of poaching, the penalties for this illegal activity being harsh:

> a man caught at night in an enclosure with instruments for trapping game could be sentenced to transportation by two magistrates, one of whom might be the injured property owner, while a blow, struck or threatened in a poaching fray, could be punished by the gallows.[4]

For the urban worker, for millions of men, women and children, the daily grind in the often dangerous factory, mill and mine was, in a word, appalling. The Factories' Inquiry Commission had shown in 1833 that many manufacturers and mine owners employed young children, and that they worked a sixteen-hour day. Moreover, flogging was regarded as part of the conditions of employment, a situation which the parents openly accepted, they having one eye on the precarious family budget. A seventy-hour working week prevailed for men, with some amelioration for women and children being introduced in stages by government legislation. Unemployment, underemployment, poverty and pauperism led to the steps of the union workhouse where conditions were deliberately made hard in order to keep out all but the most desperate. Newspapers reveal the frequent occurrence of starvation, suicides, and the terrible accidents which befell workers of all ages in their place of work, such accounts appearing in the local and provincial columns. Not until the repeal of the Corn Laws in 1846, hastened by the poor harvest of 1845 (the autumn of this year being abysmally wet), and the Irish potato famine, that the price of bread became affordable again to the mass of people. In London, to take one location, the price of a four-pound loaf was about 8d, quite a substantial amount when taken out of a weekly wage of 15s in 1841.

What of the urban areas which bore the brunt of the rural-urban migration and the rapid natural increase in population?

Those in the Midlands and the north of England, the seats of heavy industry and mining, became the foci of squalor, deprivation and all kinds of human misery:

> The appearance of such towns was dark and forbidding. Many years had now passed since the first factories appeared among the northern hills. Now the tall chimneys and gaunt mills had multiplied a hundredfold, and armies of grimy grey-slated houses were encamped around them. Overhead hung a perpetual pall of smoke so that their inhabitants groped their way to work in a fog.[5]

It was Friedrich Engels who, in 1844, stood on the Ducie Bridge in Manchester, and surveyed the scene across the valley of the polluted river Irk:

> Below the bridge you look upon piles of debris, the refuse, the filth and offal from the courts on the steep left bank; here each house is perched close behind its neighbour . . . Here the background embraces the pauper burial ground, the station of the Liverpool & Leeds Railway, and in the rear of this, the Workhouse, the 'Poor-Law Bastille' of Manchester, which like a citadel, looks threateningly down from its high walls and parapets on the hill top upon the working people's quarter below.[6]

Life for the working class was not totally encompassed by the drudgery of work. Recreation of a kind, mainly on Sundays and Christian holidays, led to such activities as rush-bearing, dog-racing, Wakes fairs, and the occasional attendance at prize-fighting. Banned activities such as the blood sports continued to draw minor crowds in secluded places. Drinking in ale houses and inns, when it could be afforded (and even when it could not), furnished some escape from the day-to-day monotony of life. The latter social evil was enhanced by the Beer House Act of 1830 which allowed the beer houses to remain open from 5 a.m. to midnight. This same Act permitted almost any house-holder who paid a small fee to sell beer, and accordingly the number of beer houses (Tom and Jerry

4. Sir Arthur Bryant, *A History of Britain and the English People*, Vol.3, p.40.

5. Ibid, pp.83/4.

6. Friedrich Engels, *The Condition of the Working Class in England*, p.89.

shops) increased. Manchester alone had, in the 1830s, nearly one thousand inns, beer houses and gin shops; Leeds had 450; and this discounts the large number of illicit stills set up by Irish cellar dwellers (Hush shops). No wonder the railway navvies who were engaged on the construction of the Manchester & Leeds Railway (or any other railway for that matter) could enjoy a binge all day on their day off; no wonder there were frequent randies, personal in-fighting and displays of aggression against rival groups.

It was also a decade of positive achievements, ranging over a variety of prodigious engineering constructions to social engineering. The first electric telegraph was tried in 1838; by an Act of 1846, the Electric Telegraph Company had been formed to exploit the new facility on a commercial basis. Not only did the railways find a ready use for it, but the invention represented just one strand in the process of bringing together peripheral and remote parts of the country. In 1839, Rowland Hill inaugurated the Penny Post, a facility at first rejected by the Post Office, but eagerly seized upon by commercial interests. No longer was the sending of mail a prerogative of the middle and ruling classes, for it could now be available to all who were literate. The Factory Act of 1844 (Graham's Act) permitted the employment of children in mining and manufacturing. Children under thirteen, however, were restricted to a 3½ hour day, with a period of schooling of three hours a day. This was a modest improvement on the Factory Act of 1833 in which provision was made for children between nine and eleven to receive two hours schooling each day. In the cotton-textile town of Rochdale, 10½ miles north east of Manchester, on the newly-formed Manchester & Leeds Railway, the first co-operative store was opened in 1844. As a self-supporting venture, it comprised 28 members of Owenite and Chartist persuasion, and it served the local populace by dint of supplying unadulterated food and drink, as well as paying dividends to its members in proportion to the amount spent.

At the end of the ten-year period, the year in which the Manchester & Leeds Railway assumed its new name of the Lancashire & Yorkshire Railway, the Ten Hours Act was introduced as a means of improving conditions of work by shortening the number of hours of labour for women and children to ten hours a day. This reduction in working hours applied only to those involved in the textile industries but as an established principle, it formed the basis upon which future acts could be introduced and extended as time progressed.

Meanwhile, the nation's incipient railway system evolved via the Stockton & Darlington Railway, which opened in 1825,[7] to a veritable scramble for Parliamentary approval of numerous railway bills, and to the subsequent acquisition of land upon which the intended railways could be laid. Of the changes which occurred during Victoria's first ten years as Queen, nothing could quite emulate the impact of the railways on the lives of ordinary people. 'No change introduced into England in the Nineteenth Century was received with such doubts and fears, none was so immediately and consistently a gain to the whole population.'[8] As if to endorse the railways as a national institution, Queen Victoria and Prince Albert travelled by train on Monday, 13 June 1842, between Slough and Paddington. This was the first journey by railway taken by the Queen (Prince Albert had already made his first journey on the 14 November 1839), and was pleased enough with the experience to travel back from Paddington to Slough on the 23 July. This was to be the beginning of many rail journeys the Queen would make as a matter of course. Unfortunately, the Manchester & Leeds Railway was never to be graced by the provision of a Royal Train. Instead, it named its Manchester station after her.

It was against this backcloth, albeit here described as a mere brush stroke of history, that the Manchester & Leeds (hereafter referred to as the M&L) was conceived and constructed, put into operation, and expanded far beyond the initial conception.

7. The Stockton & Darlington Railway could claim to be the first to carry passengers, even though by horse-drawn vehicles.

8. J.R. Green, *A Short History of the English People*, p.310.

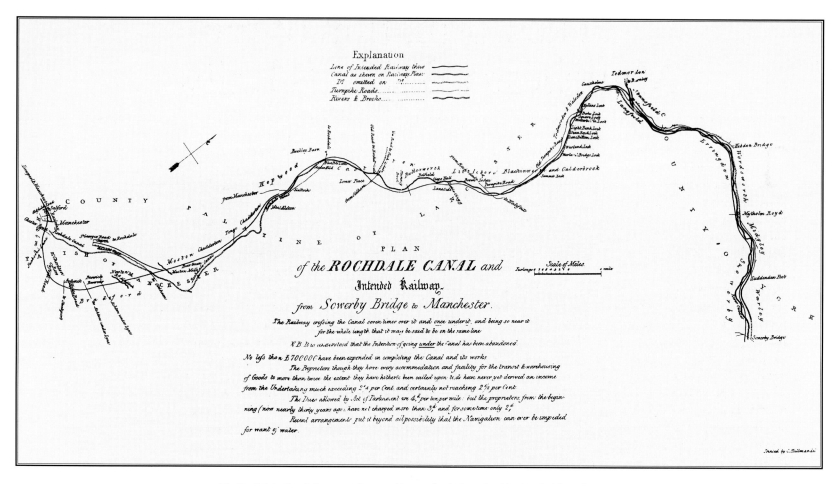

The Rochdale Canal Company drew up this map for the benefit of its shareholders who were
probably alarmed by the proposal of the railway company. Note that the intended line
of the railway at the Manchester end did not materialise as expected

TWO

The Formation of the Manchester & Leeds Railway

THE year was 1825. A group of gentlemen had formed a committee in which to consider the proposal to construct a railway between Manchester and Leeds, 'connecting as far as practicable, the towns of Rochdale, Todmorden, Halifax, Bradford and Huddersfield'. The committee comprised gentlemen from Manchester, Rochdale, Halifax, Leeds and Liverpool; subscriptions were taken, and directions to undertake surveys and all other sundries necessary for application to Parliament. After much discussion, however, the enthusiasm to proceed with the proposal was dampened and deferred. The elected committee considered the current inauspicious economic situation and came to the dismal conclusion that the whole thing would have to be postponed 'until a more favourable occasion should present itself'.[9] During these early deliberations, other projects elsewhere had been successfully launched. The Stockton & Darlington Railway had been opened for passenger traffic on 27 September 1825, having been incorporated on 19 April 1821. Nearer home, in the years following 1825, the Liverpool & Manchester Railway, incorporated on the 5 May 1826, began running its passenger trains on 15 September 1830. Other railways too had weathered the recession years: the Bolton & Leigh Railway, the Kenyon & Leigh Junction, and the Warrington & Newton. The postponement of the first proposal to link Manchester with Leeds must have been a frustrating disappointment.

The proposal lay dormant for five years. On 18 October 1830, a fresh attempt appeared to be possible, and on that date, at the Royal Hotel, Manchester, 'a highly respectable meeting' took place, Mr Samuel Brooks presiding. The prospectus looked more promising, and the *Manchester Guardian*, 30 October, reported the occasion and commented that 'In the course of the last five years, the committee have had the opportunity of observing a gradual return of general prosperity and a constantly increasing extension of commerce'. The success of the Liverpool & Manchester Company, in addition to the improved economic climate, gave new impetus to the awakened scheme. At the 18 October meeting, several resolutions were passed. The name of the new railway was to assume the title of the 'Manchester & Leeds Railway'; capital was to be raised by subscription in £100 shares, 8,000 of which were offered. Two engineers were to carry out the principal survey of the route – the eminent George Stephenson (who had just completed his work on the Liverpool & Manchester Railway), and James Walker, who had also been involved with the same. At the Manchester end, the proposed line was to form a connection with the L&M (a logical intention, but one which was to cause problems in the future), whilst at the Yorkshire end, the M&L anticipated a connection with the Leeds & Selby Railway, and with the proposed Leeds & Bradford line.

The survey done, the Bill was presented to Parliament on the 10 March 1831, in the hands of Lord Morpath. Opposition arose immediately from the Rochdale Canal Company whose waterway the line was to follow closely. Joining the opposition camp were two Yorkshire canal interests in the form of the Aire & Calder Navigation and the Calder & Hebble Company whose canal joined the Rochdale at Sowerby

9. A.F. Tait and E. Butterworth, *Views on the Manchester and Leeds Railway*, 1842.

One of the most locally-celebrated bridges which owes its origin to the M&L is the 'Iron Donger' which spans the Rochdale Canal in Chadderton, north of the Mills Hill Embankment. The bowstring bridge was taken out of use in 1904 and replaced by a new bridge alongside it. The main components of the M&L bridge are cast-iron arch ribs and the wrought-iron tie-rods joining their ends. All the remaining ironwork with the exception of the cross-girders is either secondary or ornamental. The weight of the cast iron alone is 155 tons. The sobriquet 'Iron Donger' arises from the deep sonorous tone emitted when the ironwork is struck by a heavy object. Photographed 4 October 1994 by the author

Bridge. If this was not enough, the Bill failed to receive due attention since Parliament was dissolved on the 23 April. This was to be the first débâcle in an effort to place the M&L on the statute book. The 1830 survey carried out by Stephenson and Walker laid out a route which obviated the need for expensive construction works. As the *Manchester Guardian* pointed out in its issue of 13 November: 'There will be no necessity for any tunnels, or any inclined planes, in any part of the line up which locomotive engines cannot work with advantage'. In fact, the surveys were done by each engineer independently, and both differed in their recommendations. According to Francis Whishaw: 'the line preferred by Mr Walker was that most favourable for the non-interference with valuable property, for directness, and the avoidance of tortuous lines; but it presented some gradients which would now be considered unfavourable, and a considerable length of tunnelling. The line recommended by Mr Stephenson, on the other hand, passed through some of the most luxuriant pastures, and amid some of the most valuable Mills and Factories in the West Riding of Yorkshire, and the eastern part of Lancashire, and following almost entirely the sinuosities of the Vale of Todmorden naturally presented a great variety of objectionable curves, but owing to the immense population of the district . . . it was considered upon the whole to be the most advisable plan.'[10]

An official Rochdale Canal Company plan 'of the Rochdale Canal and Intended Railway from Sowerby Bridge to Manchester' shows the 1830 route from its connection with the L&M at Oldfield Road, Salford, and then sweeping in a long curve through the districts of Hulme, Ardwick, Bradford and Newton, there to follow the Rochdale Canal throughout most of its length to Sowerby Bridge – without tunnels. The plan also reveals that a branch line, some two miles in length, left St George's Fields on the northern side of the Rochdale

10. Francis Whishaw, *Analysis of Railways*, 1842.

Canal, where a terminal station was to be erected, forming a junction with the main line at Moston Mill, in the district of Moston. At the Yorkshire end, the line was intended to run to Brighouse and there connect with the proposed Bradford & Leeds Railway, thereby giving access to the centre of the woollen empire. The length of the M&L route would have been 34 miles, between the Manchester terminus and Brighouse.

A second application to Parliament was made by the M&L board on the 22 June 1831, this time with more definite arrangements for the route between Sowerby Bridge and Leeds. The remainder of the route (west of Sowerby Bridge) remained the same, however, and the total cost was estimated to lie between £700,000 and £800,000. By a majority of 15 to 13 the Bill was again rejected on 12 July – 'the preamble not being proved' – the same implacable opponents of the Bill once more successful. Despite appearing before a Committee of Appeal, the Bill was rejected and quietly abandoned on 28 July.

In a third attempt, the M&L Company was reformed in October 1835, the proposal now appearing as a new undertaking. The long curving connection with the L&M was now deleted, the line now to run from the terminal station in St George's Field to Sowerby Bridge, and thence to Wakefield via Cooper Bridge and Dewsbury. The final part of the journey to Leeds (about nine miles) was expected to be over North Midland Railway Company metals by way of Normanton, or possibly by a parallel line. A prospectus was issued by the Directors on 1 February 1836 which gave the names of the ten directors, 'with power to add to their number'. George Stephenson remained the chief engineer; one imagines the M&L to be proud to be able to retain his name and declare it on its prospectus. As usual, in such a document, the reasons for the Bill were expounded, followed by an expatiation on the population, manufactures and anticipated traffic on the completed line. *Herapath*, March 1836, was cautiously hopeful of success with the third application to Parliament: 'There cannot be the slightest doubt but that this railway will be made sooner or later. The advantages it presents are too great for the inhabitants of Lancashire and

The railway crossed the Rochdale Canal several times between Middleton and Sowerby Bridge. This skew bridge spans the Canal at Slattocks, Middleton, and exhibits the Company's use of hand-made bricks combined with masonry. The voussoirs and parapet are dressed stone, while the surface of the arch consists of skewed brickwork. The square span is 40ft. The railway crosses the Canal obliquely – Rochdale to the left, Manchester to the right. Photographed 25 May 1997 by the author

Right: The north-eastern aspect of the same bridge, or at least one corner of it, was photographed in an attempt to show more closely the details of construction. Masonry and brickwork formed the low abutment which rises about four feet above the level of the canal; from the string course the skewed brick lining can be clearly seen. Note the corbelled masonry at the head of the buttress. A modern steel railing has been added to the parapet to afford extra protection to permanent-way staff in these safety-conscious times. Author

Yorkshire to dispense with it. Lord Stanley has consented to take charge of the Bill. Much opposition will be offered by the canal proprietors and others, and it may be doubted whether the Bill will succeed this session, but of its ultimate success there cannot be a doubt'. Whishaw states that the scheme continued to be 'violently opposed' in the House of Commons by the canal proprietors 'as well as by certain merchants and others, the Town of Leeds, as well as by several landowners along the line'.[11] The power of persuasion prevailed, however, since the opposition yielded to the final decision of the Standing Orders' Committee. The Bill passed its third reading on 21 June 1836, the Act of 6 and 7 William IV ch.3 authorising the formation of the M&L which received Royal Assent on 4 July. Section 90 of the same Act declared that the M&L's intended parallel line between Normanton and Leeds should be deferred for a period of 18 months pending the construction of the NMR's line between these two places. This the NMR did by the close of 1837 and the M&L's 'parallel line' ceased to be of consequence.

The projected line was subjected to a further survey by Messrs Stephenson and Gooch (Thomas L. Gooch having taken over from James Walker circa 1834). The *Manchester Guardian*, 1 October 1836, reported that 'We understand that the line of this railway has just been carefully re-surveyed by Mr Stephenson and Mr Gooch, with a view to improvements of the gradients and curves, and that from their report, that these will admit of very considerable alteration so as to make them decidedly superior to what was in the first instance expected'.

The re-surveyed route involved several alterations. On 9 November, application to Parliament was again made 'for powers to vary the line'. By the Act of 7 William IV ch.24, the application received Royal Assent on 5 May 1837. With this green light, there was to be no holding back the M&L Company. The complete line between the Manchester terminus and the junction at Goose Hill (three miles east of Wakefield) was 51 miles. Although circuitous, the route gave access to a number of large towns: Butterworth went so far to designate the line as 'the Eleven Towns Railway'.

Throughout the last few months of 1836 and the first part of 1837, the Directors were much engaged in the purchase of land 'at reasonable prices'. There were inevitable legal contests involved in the bargaining for land, the Company attempting to purchase at the lowest price, with the landowners and others determined to squeeze as much as possible out the Company. Such bargaining continued through 1837 and into 1838. Butterworth cites a few examples: 'the inquiry as to the value of land of property at the Warden and Fellows, Manchester, at Newton Heath, August 29th 1837 – verdict, £8,724 8s 11d; land of Henry Taylor Esq., Recorder of Pontefract, in St. George's Fields, February 6th 1838 – verdict, £17,000; manorial rights and land of James Dearden Esq., Lord of the Manor of Rochdale, at Calderbrook and Walsden, March 6th 1838 – verdict, £360 8s 9d' To a large extent, the Company came off best in these legal wrangles: 'the demands made by the landowners . . . amounted to £146,484, while the sum awarded was £4,628'.

Apart from the more civilised legal settlements, there were also more physical confrontations involving face-to-face stand-offs. The *Manchester Courier*, 8 July 1837, reported such an encounter which occurred between Mr Cawley, an M&L employee, and an irate landowner named James Leigh. Whilst Mr Cawley was engaged in marking out the line of the railway, Leigh took objection to the prospect of the railway passing through his market garden. This he did by pulling up the marking rods and intimidating Mr Cawley by using threatening language. Mr Cawley attempted to placate Leigh, but the latter expressed his determination to resist by threatening to use deadly weapons. 'Under these circumstances', wrote the *Manchester Courier*, 'Mr Cawley was obliged to proceed against him', invoking an Act for making the railway which is imposed 'on all persons who shall obstruct anyone in the legal execution of this Act.' At the Rochdale Police Offices (on a Sunday!) Leigh was fined the minimum penalty of £5 and warned by the magistrate not to impede further lest he should find himself in 'greater difficulties'. The affair had a comical side to it but was taken seriously as a warning to others who might be similarly disposed.

11. Francis Whishaw, *Analysis of Railways*, 1842.

THREE

Construction of the Main Line

Manchester to Littleborough

CONTRACT advertisements for the attention of contractors, appeared for the first time in June 1837. One of the first, which can be taken as an example, appeared in the *Manchester Guardian*, 17 June, and ran as follows:

> No.1 Contract. To make the railway with all the excavations, embankments, bridges, culverts, drains, fences, and gates complete, including the laying and ballasting of the permanent way and sidings, and furnishing the necessary blocks and sleepers (but exclusive of the rail chairs, pins and keys, and oak trenails), commencing near the Highlander Inn on the north side of a street called Junction Street, and terminating on the north west side of the occupation road to Great Nuthurst in the township of Moston . . . being a distance of about 2 miles and 64 chains.

Six contractors responded to this advertisement and offered their tenders before or on 10 July 1837. Gooch's estimate for the work was £32,000; only one contractor's tender lay below this estimate, that of Tredwell and Gerrard for £31,600, which was duly accepted on the date of return. Further contracts for the complete line between the Manchester terminus and Sowerby Bridge were later advertised in a similar manner in the press. In all, fifteen contracts were let to 'experienced and responsible contractors' between 10 July and 10 December 1838.

Construction of the line commenced on 18 August 1837, although Butterworth states the 'The first breaking of the ground at Slack's Valley in Chadderton'[12] took place on the following day. By the 26 August, the *Manchester Courier* was able to inform its readers that:

> This extensive undertaking has been commenced at three points on the line in the neighbourhood of Oldham, namely, opposite the Three Crowns Inn, Newton Heath; in the valley at Moston Mill; and near Royle Farm, Castleton. The road from Manchester to the neighbourhood of Oldham and Rochdale will probably be complete in a few months and before any other part of the line is materially proceeded with.

The contractors worked under heavy penalties to complete their contracts by May 1839 and it was anticipated in the Hunt's Bank board room that the line between Manchester and Rochdale 'would be in a fit state to be opened'. 'The prospects of remuneration to the shareholders are most cheering', commented *Herapath's Journal* in October 1837, 'and quite justify the very favourable opinion with which the public regards this important railway'. A few details of how the work at the Manchester end of the line were given at a Committee of Management meeting on 9 August 1838. Of the six contracts between the terminus and the Summit Tunnel, the general progress was described as 'going on satisfactorily', leaving only the Manchester Viaduct behind schedule, 'a great deal of stone on the ground'.[13] *The Railway*

12. Edwin Butterworth, *Historical Sketch of the Manchester and Leeds Railway*, 1839.

13. PRO RAIL 343/485.

Few of the 58 arches which carried the railway into Oldham Road Station remain today. This section of eleven arches stands adjacent to New Allen Street; the nearer end has been truncated where it originally passed over a street and is now supported by a modern brick abutment. At the farther end the viaduct linked up with a stone wall which partly surrounded the M&L Miles Platting Locomotive Works. Author

The date 1836 on this gradient list suggests an early survey of the proposed line possibly carried out by Stephenson or Gooch. It includes the final stretch between Goose Hill, Normanton, and Leeds, hence the distance of 60 miles 50 chains. Unfortunately, the list does not differentiate between rising or falling gradients (Public Record Office)

The asymmetrical gradient profile (far right) of the 51 mile route between Manchester and Normanton is based on L&Y surveys. The steep rise up the western side of the Pennines contrasts with the long and more gradual ascent from the east. Little correlation exists between this and the gradient list

Times, 30 March 1839, adverted to an Engineer's report given by Stephenson and Gooch.

> The whole of the works, consisting of excavations, embankments, bridges, culverts, and the laying of the permanent way, are in such an advanced state between Manchester and Littleborough, that there can be no doubt of this portion of the line being ready for opening in the month of May next . . . The viaduct at Manchester is nearly completed, excepting that portion required for the stations, sidings, etc, and it is now arranged to proceed, without delay, with the extension of the arches up to Lees Street, and to make provision for the arrival and departure of passengers . . . The whole quantity of earthwork between Manchester and Littleborough is 2,107,360 cubic yards and out of this quantity there is executed 2,043,360, leaving only 64,000 cubic yards of earthwork to be executed.

In addition to the 730 yard Manchester Viaduct there were two major earthworks alluded to in the above report. One at Moston Cutting, about three miles from the terminus, and which was described by Butterworth as 'an exceedingly heavy cutting' in clay, and of 'a slippery tendency'. This was a thick and sticky yellow/blue boulder clay of glacial origin which, along with sands and gravels, smothered an extensive area north of Manchester. One imagines the overburden removed from this cutting was transferred further along the line towards Mills Hill where it was necessary to carry the line on a long embankment across the shallow but wide valley of the Irk. In the course of building the embankment it was necessary to construct a substantial culvert which could convey the river through from one side to the other. This was achieved by laying the two-arch tunnels 'on concrete of the best materials, viz, Ardwick lime and screened gravel got on the spot'.[14] Butterworth described the embankment as 'about the highest railway embankment in England, having an average height of 40 feet, with a maximum height of 70 feet, yet so carefully has it been made that it is said to have sunk

5 feet since its construction'.[15] An estimated 319,202 cubic yards of earth was used in the embankment and such was the rate of progress in its formation that 40,000 cubic yards of earth had been removed from one location, carried, and deposited in the space of one month – this achievement receiving official recognition. Not that this sort of achievement should hide the fact that not everything went according to plan smoothly, or as expected during the line's construction. The *Manchester Courier*, 21 October 1837, referred to the Mills Hill embankment where work was proceeding 'night as well as day', and where

> Small waggons drawn by one horse each and constructed upon a new method so as to contain about three cubic yards of earth are extensively employed, and they are found to facilitate the works in a material degree . . . one of the workmen was injured on Friday last by an accident on the line; he got betwixt two waggons, and was crushed; he was removed to his residence at Middleton and by prompt medical aid has been rescued from danger.

At the Manchester end of the line, the Company had been experiencing problems regarding compensation to the owners of land adjacent to the Manchester Viaduct. The *Manchester Courier*, 7 July 1838, furnished the full details of an inquiry

> to assess the amount of compensation to be paid by the Manchester and Leeds Railway Company to the

Totally ignored by those who live close by, or who travel above them, are two 8ft span arched culverts which convey the Irk beneath the Mills Hill Embankment. No effort was spared to construct these relatively minor passages for a river which has been known to flood the surrounding area in times of torrential rain. This aspect is the side facing west towards Middleton; the culvert is built with stone facing and brickwork, dressed stone being used for the curved wing wall on the right-hand side. The eastern side is virtually impossible to reach without trespassing. Photographed 10 April 1997 by the author

> owners of the Roman Catholic School and Nunnery, near the station of the Company, in Oldham Road. The Company required 267 yards of land belonging to the school, and the inquiry was as to the amount to be paid for that land, and the damage which would ensue to the institution in consequence of the vicinity of the railway.

In this affair, the Company had offered £111 for the land and nothing for damages. It was another example of the Company

14. *Manchester Courier*, 9 December 1837.

15. Edwin Butterworth, *Historical Sketch of the Manchester and Leeds Railway*, 1839.

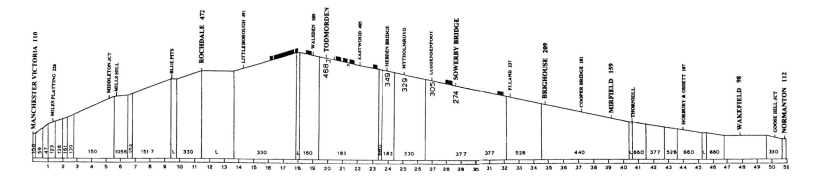

The building shown here corresponds with the station building at Rochdale in Tait's lithograph (see page 46). From the front of the railway office there projected a canopy supported on six posts, under which waiting passengers could seek shelter. This is the M&L 'railway office' in August 1956, by then used as a permanent-way gang's retreat. The missing stucco reveals a wall of hand-made bricks, whilst similar brickwork can be seen in the gable-end wall and chimney stacks. Author's Collection

16. *Manchester Courier*, 11 August 1838.

17. M&L Board Minutes, 19 November 1838.

18. The river Roch appears as 'Roach' on its arrival in the vicinity of Bury; the two engineers were probably unaware of this subtle difference.

19. Francis Whishaw, *The Railways of Great Britain and Ireland*, 1842.

20. PRO RAIL 343/485.

21. Tait and Butterworth, *Views of the Manchester and Leeds Railway*, p.14.

22. Butterworth, *Historical Sketch of the Manchester & Leeds Railway*, p.9.

attempting to have its own way at the least expense, regardless of the rights of the landowner. In the final outcome, the latter received a total of £499 3s 4d.

Further up the line at Rochdale, there was trouble with a gang of Irish navvies who were employed on the Rochdale Contract. Late on a Sunday evening in August 1838, the men, 'armed with all kinds of deadly weapons', wandered the streets of the town and assaulted everybody they met'. Once they were held in check, three of the gang were hauled before the magistrates and fined; two, in default of paying, were sent to prison for two months.[16] If the Irish had already forged for themselves a bad name, they continued to do so. The *Manchester Guardian*, 13 October 1838, gave news of a turn-out of navvies:

> On Monday, in consequence of a dispute betwixt one of the subcontractors and a times-man, the whole of the Irishmen working at the Mills Hill embankment, struck work, and after a short cessation, returned of their own accord. On Wednesday night, the contractors paid off the whole of the hands without distinction and discharged them, and they remained out of work all Thursday. It was expected, however, that a rearrangement would take place yesterday or today, the Irish hands excepted.

The Company had run into trouble in the previous month in connection with construction allegedly having taken place on Sundays. Under a banner headline, 'Profanation of the Sabbath', the *Manchester Guardian*, 26 September, highlighted the employment of navvies on Sunday work, to which the Directors replied by stating that Sunday working was against their instructions, and to ensure that this practice was not undertaken, they had a year before inserted a clause into all contracts. This had imposed a penalty of £50 'on any contractor who should carry out his work on a Sunday'. So anxious were the contractors to complete the line within the terms of their contract that the incidence of Sunday working was probably ignored until brought to the attention of the Company. According to Board Minutes, the penalty clause against Sunday working did not apply to the Moston Cutting contract, but was inserted into all contracts subsequently.[17] Despite these and other difficulties, construction of the line actually reached beyond Littleborough to a point within 180 yards of the *pièce de résistance*, the Summit Tunnel. A report given by Stephenson and Gooch on 30 March 1839, referred to the advanced state of the works, and to the infant river Roch as it trickled its way over the aqueduct: 'The Roach brook,[18] which is taken over the railway near the tunnel entrance, can be made to answer the purpose of a watering place for the engines'.

By the close of 1840, five stations had been erected: the Manchester terminus, Mills Hill, Blue Pits, (Castleton), Rochdale, and Littleborough. Whishaw, writing in 1842, described the terminus as being 'situate between Lees Street and St. George's Street', the lines approaching the station carried 'entirely on arches'. Whishaw continued, 'The passenger shed is covered with a wooden roof in two spans. The booking office is on the ground floor; and the passenger platform is approached by a flight of forty five steps each of $7\frac{1}{2}$ inches rise. The whole length of the station is 176 yards, and the width 80 yards.'[19] At Rochdale, ten miles from Manchester, the line ran through the periphery of the town (originally a branch was to be laid to the town, connecting with the main line, but this was abandoned owing to the expected inconvenience in operations). After the opening of the line between Manchester and Littleborough, Butterworth focused his attention on the town and the anticipated benefits which the railway would bring to the people:

> By means of the railway, the inhabitants of Rochdale are brought within twenty minutes distance of Manchester, and no doubt they will soon discover and experience the advantages which this practically nearer neighbourhood will give to the great market for their manufactures, and the great centre of the business and commerce of the district.

The construction of the Rochdale Station had been placed in the hands of David Bellhouse Junior, at a cost of £1,100, 'to be partially finished for the transaction of business by the 25th May inst'.[20] Butterworth commented that it 'is a commodious and neat edifice well-adapted for the accommodation of passengers'.[21] The three lesser stations, Mills Hill, Blue Pits, and Littleborough also deserve mention. Mills Hill was sited close to and to the south of the famous embankment. It served the people of Middleton, Royton, Chadderton and Oldham, being just over two miles by road from the latter town. It ranked as the first stopping place out of Manchester and was Oldham's station until the Oldham Branch was opened on 31 March 1842 between Middleton Junction and Werneth. Blue Pits station was given but a brief mention in the *Manchester Courier*, 12 October 1839, the station being the location of a fatal accident to a labourer, who, while drunk, had decided to walk to Middleton, his home town, from Littleborough along the railway. The newspaper remarked that 'it is the first fatal accident on the line since it was opened'. On 21 October, the newspaper again referred to the station in connection with a separate incident as 'Heywood Bridge Station', the inference being that the early station carried two names.

Seemingly as important as Rochdale, a few miles further on, Littleborough had the distinction of being the ephemeral terminus, and as 'the most distant place from Manchester to which trains pass as yet'.[22] It was at the Littleborough station that horse-drawn coaches enabled travellers to reach Todmorden and Hebden Bridge via the turnpike road. The

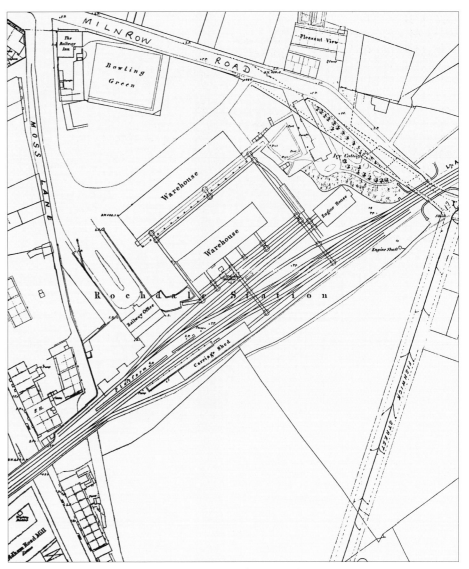

Manchester Courier, 6 July 1839, provided a brief glimpse of the unfinished station: 'The building, which is about 50 yards long, and 20 in width, is as yet only roofed on one side', while *Herapath*, 20 July, adds that 'we may observe that it stands on a viaduct of considerable height, having a flight of stairs up the side of the viaduct, with booking offices, waiting rooms, etc, below the level of the line'.

Rochdale Station, circa 1851. The station under the control of the L&Y would not have changed much since M&L days a few years earlier

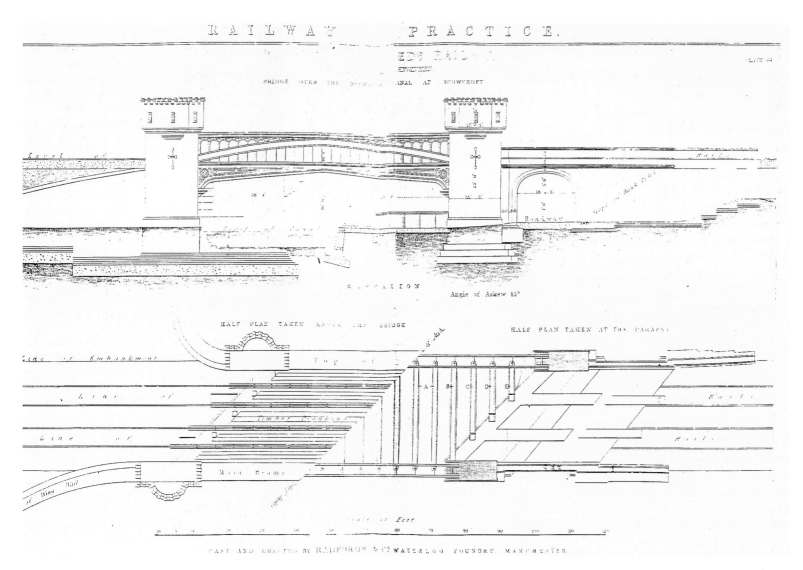

Elevation, plan and half-plan of the skew bridge at Scowcroft, Middleton.
Although still standing, the bridge has long been abandoned and now remains as a
monument to the civil engineering prowess of the M&L

Sowerby Bridge to Todmorden

ONTRACTS for the eastern section of the main line were advertised during 1838. Taking the extremities of the section, the following contract advertisements appeared in the *Manchester Guardian*, 2 May, and in *Herapath*, September 1838, respectively:

> Sowerby Contract, including the Sowerby Tunnel . . . commencing in the field No.172, Sowerby township, situated between Longbottom Mill and Hollings Mill, and terminating opposite the gas works in Sowerby Bridge, being a distance of about 1 mile and a quarter. Winterbut Lee Contract, to make and maintain the railway and a diversion of the Rochdale Canal . . . commencing near the east end of the Summit Tunnel, at a footpath in field No.80, Todmorden and Walsden township, and terminating at the junction with the Todmorden Contract, a point about five chains to the north east of Clough Mill, being a distance of about 1 mile 17 chains.

Certain landowners in Todmorden were equally keen to extract the maximum compensation from the Company as those between Manchester and Rochdale. One of the most powerful and influential in this respect came in the form of Messrs Fielden of Todmorden, the major textile concern in the town and surrounding area. The *Manchester Courier*, 13 October 1838, gave details of the sheriff's court proceedings which occupied two days.

> Messrs Joshua, John, James and Thomas Fielden claimed compensation for a piece of land 300 yards in length by 50 feet in breadth . . . Mr James Holt, surveyor, Todmorden, estimated the total amount of compensation at £1,819 13s 10d . . . The jury, after nearly an hour's consultation, gave their verdict, assessing the damages as follows – land and buildings and timber, £1,191 10s 6d; severance, including £55 mill damages, £215.

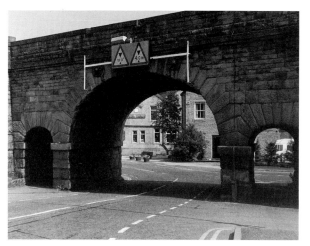

Thomas Fielden was a director of the M&L Railway, but despite this commitment, his first responsibility was to the family textile business. A similar situation occurred at Sowerby Bridge, in which the railway company was at odds with a Samuel Turner, landowner. *The Railway Times*, 12 January 1839, had its man at the proceedings which were held at the Northgate Hotel, Halifax. 'The property in dispute is situated at Sowerby Bridge not far from the vitriol works, and was stated to contain a valuable stone quarry. The sum asked was £1,500 and the tender made by the Company was £500, which did not take into account the stone, but merely the value of the land.' The jury was out for ninety minutes before returning and awarding the sum of £475 to be paid by the Company to Mr Turner. This amount being less than the offer made by the Company, Mr Turner had to pay the costs!

There were mixed fortunes with the work in the eastern section. This was referred to in the Engineer's Report given on 18 March 1839:

> The Winterbut Lee Contract, which is next to the tunnel, is going on satisfactorily. The Gauxholme Viaduct, considering the difficulties encountered by the contractor not obtaining possession of the land, is proceeding satisfactorily, and there is every reason to believe, that by ordinary exertion, will be completed at the time specified. The Todmorden Contract, owing

Littleborough Station is built on the eight-arch Littleborough Viaduct. Arch No.7 forms the 28ft 6in. skewed span over the A58 Rochdale to Halifax road, to this day a major traffic hazard owing to the narrowness of the road and its position near to two road junctions. The construction of the bridge led to litigation on account of the alleged departure from the original M&L plans in August 1839. One unusual feature of the bridge are two arches spanning the footpaths, one each side of the road. The bridge illustrates that the construction of the railway on a straight course took precedence over the alignment of the road which was forced to assume the sharp bend and narrow highway which led to so much contention in 1839. Photographed 4 August 1997 by the author

The viaduct at Mytholmroyd is a difficult one to photograph. From the path which leads up to the Up platform of the station, it is possible to achieve this view of the southern aspect of the five arches. Of all the viaducts still in use on the line, this one appears to be the least well-maintained. Above the concrete capping is a timber fence supported by scaffolding, a BR expediency perpetuated by Railtrack. Tie-bar plates stud the viaduct showing evidence of strengthening in the past. Photographed 4 August 1997 by the author

to the same causes which impeded the Gauxholme Viaduct, namely, not obtaining possession of the land in time, is in a backward state, and will require all the energy of the contractor in order to enable him to complete his contract by the time stipulated . . . The works on the Charlestown Contract . . . are of such a nature that there is no difficulty in completing them by the time stipulated (This was premature optimism as will be seen later). The Mytholmroyd Contract, although only recently commenced, is proceeding in a satisfactory manner. The Luddenden Foot Contract

is not proceeding quite so rapidly as could be wished, but as the material has to be carried to form embankments at each end of the excavation, there is no doubt of its being finished in time.

As can be seen from the above, Stephenson and Gooch had to be adept, when reporting to the Directors and shareholders, in keeping them satisfied with good news, and softening that which was not so promising. Whenever problems arose, optimism prevailed. It was impossible to be sanguine about the loss of life. The *Manchester Guardian*, from its far-off position in Manchester, reported a fatality on 18 May:

> On Friday evening a shocking accident occurred at the excavation for the tunnel of the Manchester and Leeds Railway in Walsden, near Todmorden. A large quantity of stone suddenly loosened and fell upon five workmen. One of them was killed on the spot and the others seriously injured.

The name of the tunnel was not given, but its location in Walsden suggests the Winterbut Lee Tunnel.

The summer months were the most pleasant months for the navvies to work in. During hot spells of weather, they assuaged their thirsts with bouts of drinking, and the heat

Gauxholme skew bridge as seen from the elevated ground on the northern side of the railway. This view shows the bridge in perspective: that is, forming a link between the seventeen-arch Gauxholme No.1 Viaduct and the four-arch Gauxholme No.2 Viaduct of which the bridge is the first opening. Author

Probably the most well-known of the M&L structures on the entire line
is the skew bridge over the Rochdale Canal at Gauxholme, west of Todmorden.
The original 91ft 2in. skew span consisted of cast-iron girders which were manufactured in 1840 by the
iron founders J. Butler & Co., of Stanningley, Leeds. Strengthening by additional girders took place in 1906, and these
can be seen beneath the original ironwork. The stone abutments were embellished with two castellated buttresses
at each end of the bridge, making the structure one of the most impressive features of the entire railway.
The view was taken in the summer of 1996 from the Todmorden side by the author

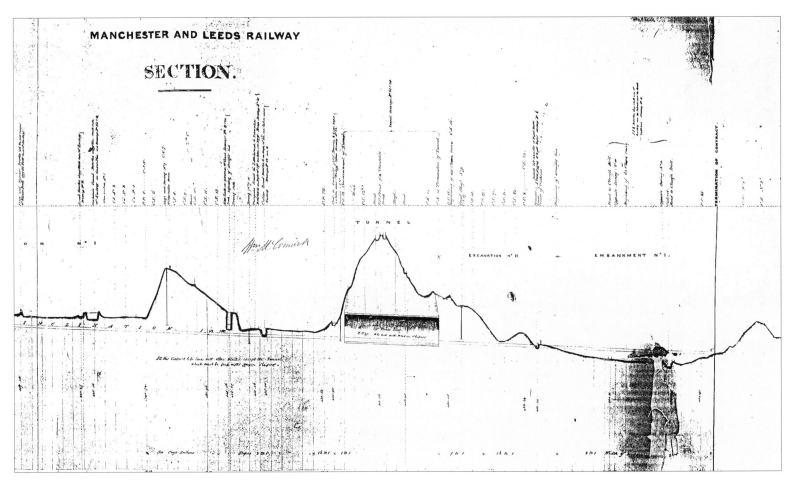

MANCHESTER AND LEEDS RAILWAY

SECTION.

Winterbutlee Tunnel formed part of William McCormick's contract. The diagram shows the eastern end of his contract

would fire up short tempers which might lead to disputes being settled by fisticuffs. Rochdale had had its rampant navvies making nuisances of themselves; so too did bucolic Hebden Bridge. The *Manchester Courier*, 27 July 1839, reported 'desperate affrays' between Irish and English labourers, a disagreement about wages being sufficient to spark off trouble: 'About 100 English labourers commenced an attack on about the same number of Irish labourers for the express purpose of driving the latter from their employment, on alleged ground that the Irish were working for lower wages' The disturbance lasted a full day and with such ferocity that many injuries were sustained on both sides. With the

assistance of the military, 'the disturbances were suppressed', only for them to recommence the following day with increased numbers and passion. 'Another attachment of military from Todmorden hastened to the spot, and by their timely interference, order was once again restored.' This newspaper took a dim view of railway workmen in general and strongly supported the need 'of establishing effective police along all extensive railways'.

Further references to the rate of progress of the works on the eastern section appeared in Engineer's reports and in the pages of the press. The route of the railway to the north and east of Walsden involved expensive and difficult engineering

Three stone-arch tunnels were necessary to bear the railway through tongues of high ground to the east of Todmorden. The first was the 225yd Millwood Tunnel (above) of which the photograph shows the eastern end. Note the curved wing walls and the high parapet. The 194yd Castle Hill Tunnel (below) follows a short distance further east, its western mouth exhibiting massive buttresses. The third tunnel is the 274yd Horsfall Tunnel (top left) of which the eastern portal reveals much distortion in its profile due to ground movements.

These photographs taken in 1951/2 by David Ibbotson.

features, confined as it was to the sinuous valleys of Walsden Water (Todmorden Valley) and the upper Calder, and having to share the limited space with the existing Rochdale Canal and the turnpike road. By the beginning of September 1839, Stephenson and Gooch were able to report the following:

> Gauxholme viaduct contract – this work is very nearly finished. Todmorden and Millwood contracts – the principal features of these contracts are, a large embankment across the Burnley valley [that is, the Calder valley as it forms an elbow curve at Todmorden], a large iron bridge over the Rochdale Canal, and the Castle Hill tunnel. The embankment consists of 364,000 cubic yards of which 190,000 are already executed. The bridge is in progress, and is to be completed by May next. The Castle Hill tunnel is proceeding favourably. Some slips have occurred in the cuttings but as material is required for the embankment, they are not of very great importance.

During these extensive activities, the Charlestown and Horsfall tunnels were under construction. The same report refers to the satisfactory progress being made on the tunnels, as well as the nearby Horsefall and Whiteley's viaducts where 'the masonry of both viaducts is in progress', and that 'the Whiteley viaduct includes a crossing of the Rochdale Canal, the ironwork for which is be erected in the early part of the summer of next year'.

At the far end of the eastern section, at Sowerby Bridge, all seemed to be going well. *The Railway Times*, 30 November 1839, found space amongst a myriad of newsworthy items to announce that

> We are happy that the spirited contractor for the tunnel at Sowerby Bridge, Mr Fraser, will have the pleasure to find that a greater part of his arduous undertaking will be

Left: On the western approach to Hebden Bridge, motorists have to negotiate the curve of the A646 road as it sweeps beneath Whiteley's Viaduct. Two of the 25ft wide arches form part of the highway, leaving one of the arches as a car park and rubbish dump for a nearby petrol station. The plainness of this viaduct may contrast with the nearby ornate skew bridge at Gauxholme, but still has a measure of attraction when compared to the monotonous brick arches of the Manchester Viaduct. Photographed 4 August 1997 by the author

Below left: Lobb Mill Viaduct stands on the eastern side of Hebden Bridge. Its purpose appears to be to maintain the gradient of the railway, the course of which hugs the edge of steep-sided ground. Unlike the Todmorden Viaduct, Lobb Mill Viaduct does not bear the railway over a river valley. Photographed 29 May 1997 by the author

Below: Gothic relieving arches at the base of the eastern abutment of Lobb Mill Viaduct

completed this day by a complete junction of the Shafts No.2 and No.3. This, we understand, is the first complete junction yet obtained on the unopened part of this railway and reflects the highest credit on the skill and ingenuity of the contractor.

Some of the heaviest works on the eastern section were found between the Summit Tunnel and Hebden Bridge. The winter of late 1839 and early 1840 was particularly punishing, and caused delays in the work owing to the unstable nature of the sodden ground in the deep cuttings and on the steep embankments. Masonry work was little hindered, however, as this had been done during the dry months of 1839. By the early summer of 1840, contractors, navvies, and the inhabitants of Todmorden had something to celebrate. The *Manchester Guardian*, 23 May, ever cognisant of events far and near, focused some attention on the Todmorden Viaduct:

> Thursday last witnessed the passing of the first waggon over the viaduct at Todmorden, the first stone of which was laid on the 21st February 1839. It consists of nine arches, seven of which are of 60 feet span each, and two of which 30 feet; the height from the surface of the turnpike road leading to Burnley to the level of the permanent rails is 54 feet 6 inches. The viaduct is built wholly of the best stone for which the district is justly celebrated; and its appearance is extremely noble and striking, reflecting great credit not only upon the engineer, but also upon the contractors, Messrs Hiram, Craven and Sons.

Whilst success prevailed along the eastern section, with an early promise of opening for public use, the one fly in the ointment occurred at Charlestown, between Todmorden and Hebden Bridge. Here, as part of the Charlestown Contract, Gooch's estimate for a tunnel had been set at £96,000; there was some debate, however, involving Gooch and Gill (the Managing Director) as to the relative costs of a tunnel and an open cutting. Board Minutes of 10 December 1838 indicate that Thomas Harding and John Cropper's tender of

£96,413, might be reduced by dint of constructing an open cutting instead of a tunnel. Any work in this area had been delayed due to non-possession of land,[23] and in the end, Harding and Cropper were authorised to proceed with a tunnel. This caused problems from the start. As fast as the bore was excavated, the loose, friable, sandy strata collapsed. On 8 June 1840, Mr Gill reported that the masonry inside 'had given way from the extra pressure of the hill', and he suggested a diversion, 'round the hill as a temporary expedient'.[24] Stephenson and Gooch also referred to the problem in their report of 10 September 1840, reluctantly admitting that this was one tunnel which would not be completed at the same time as the other works.

> We have determined, therefore, for the present, to carry the line round the hill by curves of about 12 chains radius, and for a length of about 300 yards, which, though objectionable, and involving some extra power, will be passed safely at a moderate speed. This detour of the line by the adoption of curves above described, can be made at a very moderate expense.

Gooch did not expect the temporary line to be needed for more than three or four months.[25] Although not anticipated at the time, the detour was to remain a permanent one.

There were four stations erected between the unfinished Summit Tunnel and Sowerby Bridge by the end of 1840: Todmorden, Hebden Bridge, Eastwood, and Luddenden Foot. Of Todmorden, Eastwood and Luddenden Foot, nothing seems to have caught the attention of Butterworth, Whishaw, or the press. Hebden Bridge evidently did catch Butterworth's eye

The approach to Sowerby Bridge was preceded by passage through a tunnel of the same name, 657 yards long, and as straight as a die. This elegant portal shows yet another style fashioned by the contractor's masons. All tunnels along the line had either semi-circular or elliptical-arch profiles: this tunnel fell into the former category.
Another study in tunnel architecture captured by David Ibbotson in 1951

23. M&L Board Minutes, 4 April 1839.

24. Ibid, 8 June 1840.

25. PRO RAIL 343/485.

Right: Weasel Hall Tunnel was of unusual design as can be seen in this view of the western portal. The arch was circular in cross-section, the length of the tunnel reaching 109 yards. Built on a curve, the railway passed under a minor road which led from Hebble End to Erringden, hence the need for a battered wing-wall to the height of the tunnel parapet and the high retaining wall supporting the road above.
This photograph was taken by David Ibbotson in 1951

for he described the station as 'one of the neatest stations on the entire line'.[26] Sowerby Bridge quickly assumed the role as an important railway centre, and again Butterworth waxed lyrical on observing the station: 'an extremely neat edifice, built on a sort of old English style, as it were, of ornamental, half-timbered materials, with a spacious shed for goods, a little beyond'.[27] Sowerby Bridge had the distinction of being roughly equidistant between Manchester and Leeds, being 28 miles from the former and 32 from the latter.

Goose Hill Junction to Sowerby Bridge

SEVERAL contracts were let for this lengthy (22½ miles) section of the main line. Marshall[28] furnishes a complete list of contractors for the project, those applying to the east of Sowerby Bridge appearing thus:

Copley: Tredwell & Gerrard, 11 March 1838.
Elland: James Jennings, 17 September 1838.
Rastrick: John Woodward, 10 December 1838.
Cooper Bridge: John Tomkinson, 25 June 1838.
Mirfield: William McCormick & John Crowther, 11 June 1838.
Thornhill: John Tomkinson, 25 June 1838.
Horbury: J.B. & M. Faviell, 20 November 1837.

Wakefield: Hattersley & Smith, 9 April 1838.
Kirkthorpe: Hugh McKintosh, 4 December 1837.

All but one of these contracts appeared in the press as contract advertisements soliciting tenders; the Kirkthorpe Contract appears not to have been advertised (The *Manchester Guardian*, *Leeds Mercury*, and the *Wakefield Journal* omitting this particular contract). As can be seen, however, Hugh McKintosh offered an acceptable tender (£46,000) and was engaged on the Kirkthorpe Contract. McKintosh was very much involved in the civil engineering projects east of Wakefield as well as at Goole. His name is not only

26. Tait and Butterworth, ibid., p.21.

27. Ibid, p.24.

28. John Marshall, *The Lancashire & Yorkshire Railway*, Vol.1, p.40.

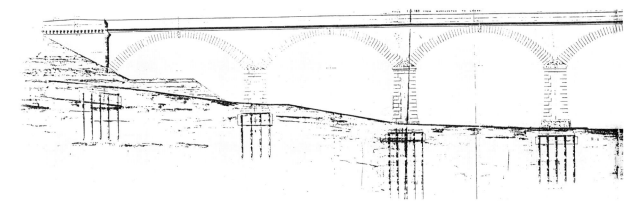

associated with the railway at Kirkthorpe but also with works on the Aire & Calder Navigation. Of more anon.

Between Walsden and Sowerby Bridge, the railway engineers had to deal with tunnels and viaducts in order to secure the railway within the confines of the narrow valleys of Walsden Water and the river Calder. To the east of Sowerby Bridge, the Calder Valley gradually broadens and gives more scope for laying a railway. Even so, it was necessary to excavate two tunnels, at Elland – 420 yards, and at Horbury, plus a number of viaducts at Rastrick, Mirfield and Wakefield, and to excavate at least four deep cuttings near Brighouse, Bradley Wood, Sowerby Bridge and Horbury. Because of the meanderings of the Calder, it was also necessary to build ten bridges, many of them two- or three-arch structures. Horbury Tunnel was necessary because of the loose shale and the presence of old coal workings. It was opened out in 1900 to form a continuous cutting, when widening for four lines.

Reports in the press and in contemporary journals provide an on-going up-date of the levels of progress (or otherwise) at various locations. Take, for example, the start of work at Mirfield. *The Railway Times*, 28 July 1838, observed a busy scene:

The contractors for making the Manchester and Leeds Railway through Mirfield are beginning their operations. This, with the canal being drawn off, for the purposes of being cleaned out, and the farmers being busy in the hay field, causes all labourers to be pretty well

employed at present. It is supposed that the railway will cause a good deal of work for the next three years, especially to masons as it will cross the river at several places, and one of these bridges will have to be a large one, spanning over two mill goits and the road, as well as at the river at Ledgard Bridge.

Stephenson and Gooch, reporting on 9 September 1839, commented that 'Between Hebden Bridge and Wakefield, the Sowerby, Elland and Cooper Bridge Contracts are those containing the heaviest works', but anticipated their completion by 'the autumn of 1840'.

The Cooper Bridge Contract consists of two large bridges over the River Calder, one of which is well-advanced, and the other is in progress. About 17,000 cubic yards remains to be done on this contract, but as it will be brought into the embankment at each end there is no difficulty in completing it.

The tone of optimism, however, covered a number of real problems. As with other sections of the line, there were difficulties with land and property owners, and not least with the Aire & Calder, and the Calder & Hebble Canal companies. In May 1838 there had been disputes over land in the Thorns Lane area of Wakefield, and also in the Kirkthorpe area, east of the town. Both disputes over compensation for loss of land and damages to property went in favour of the Company in

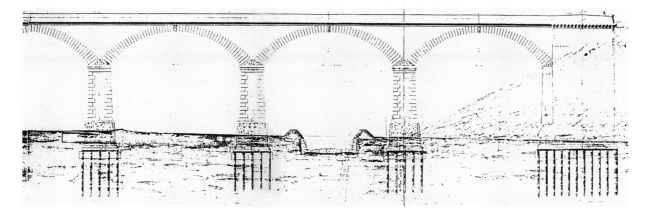

This contractor's drawing of the Todmorden Viaduct shows the timber piling which supported each pier. Not shown is the fact that the piers were wedge-shaped to effect the smooth curve of the structure. The view is towards the concave front of the viaduct which faces south east, with the embanked river Calder passing through the penultimate eastern arch

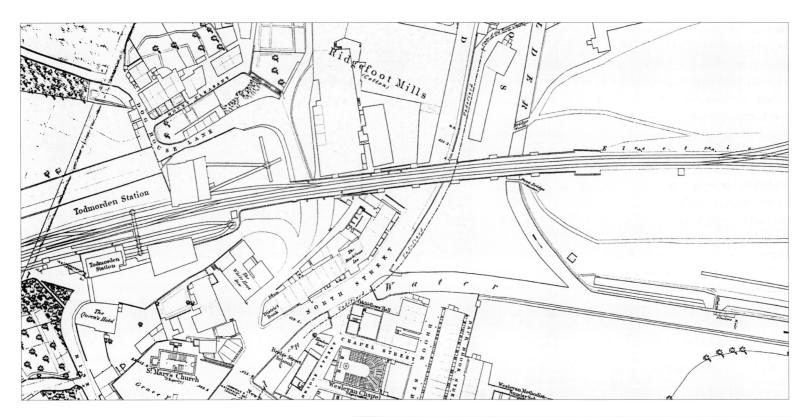

Above: Todmorden Station and Viaduct in 1852. Note the proximity of the Queen's Hotel to the station, to which it was connected by a covered footbridge for the convenience of travellers

Right: Looking west from a magnificent three-arch stone bridge, east of Sowerby Bridge, it is possible to gain an idea of the depth and width of the western end of Sowerby Bridge Cutting. The gradient of the line at this point is 1 in 274, falling towards Elland (behind the camera). As in the case of the Moston Cutting, four miles from Manchester, there is as much cutting to the east of the bridge as can be seen here. *Herapath* refers to the cutting as 'one of the deepest and extensive cuttings on the line, the greatest depth being eighty feet below the surface', and one excavated in a mixture of hard rock and shale. Photographed 4 August 1997 by the author

court settlements. Worse was to follow. The Company had in its Act secured the right to construct a viaduct in Wakefield, on its approach to the station. This had been partially built when the local inhabitants, especially the most affected by the railway, and probably with the covert support of the Navigation Company, placed an injunction on the railway company to prevent it continuing. This was in April 1839. A number of court cases took place between August 1838 and March 1840, the legal wrangles fought around the claim that the viaduct had been built with two of its piers occupying a part of the highway (Kirkgate) so contracting the width of the road from 34 feet to 30 feet. Matters became so inflamed that the railway company was expecting to demolish the viaduct as part of a compromise with the Wakefield petitioners!

The Wakefield inhabitants, allegedly backed by the Navigation Company, must have thought that their wishes had been granted by divine providence for, on 9 November 1838, a part of the viaduct collapsed. The *Manchester Guardian*, 13 November, gave a full report of the incident:

> On Thursday morning an accident attended with loss of life happened in Kirkgate in Wakefield as a waggon loaded with rubbish was passing over a line of brick arches adjoining the western end of the viaduct. Two of them gave way with an instantaneous and tremendous crash. Nine men, and a boy, who were driving the horse attached to the waggon fell with the ruins, and one man, James Williams, was so seriously crushed as to leave but faint hopes for his recovery . . . It is apparent that the adjoining arches have sustained such a shake as to render the utmost caution necessary in approaching them.

During the next twelve months the Company continued with the construction and reconstruction of the viaduct, undaunted by the litigation and captious attitude of the local people. The *Wakefield Journal*, 18 October 1839, a champion of the Wakefield petitioners, could not hide its consternation:

> We are told that workmen are completing the viaduct over Kirkgate; from which circumstance we are led to

presume that some arrangement has been entered into between the contending parties . . . We have understood that the affair was not to have been settled by a jury in a superior court and such may be the case notwithstanding the present operations.

The newspaper was correct for as late as March 1840, at the York Spring Assizes, it was still being argued that the viaduct had not been built by the Company 'in conformity with the provisions of their Act'. In turn the Company averred that if this was the case, 'the whole of their viaduct would have to be pulled down and rebuilt at immense cost and sacrifice of time', and if one arch should be substituted for three,

> it would also occasion great inconvenience as it would be necessary if only one span was allowed, that the crown of the arch should be ten or twelve feet higher than the present level of the line and therefore considerable alterations in the gradients would be occasioned.[29]

To vindicate the Company's stance in the matter, the final verdict fell in favour of the Company, which had done no wrong in the construction of their viaduct. Thus it remained as built.

An equally vexatious problem concerned the crossing of the river Calder three times at a place called Broad Reach, north east of Wakefield. From as early as January 1839 the

The last tunnel on the approach to Wakefield was located at Horbury, about 2 miles to the south west of the city. As far as is known no photographic record exists which shows the character of the tunnel. Owing to this, as at other locations, resort has had to be made to a present-day view, in this case, of where the tunnel used to be. The 128yd long tunnel was opened out by the L&Y in preparation for the widening of the line between Horbury and Wakefield in 1903. Horbury Wood bridge can be seen spanning the cutting some distance away. Photographed 11 April 1997 by the author

29. *The Railway Times*, 21 March 1840.

Elland Tunnel was the pen-ultimate tunnel on the M&L line between Littleborough and Wakefield. Although this is a view taken in L&Y days, the eastern (or station) end of the 420yd tunnel remained as built, adorned with a corbelled cornice and with rounded voussoirs. Close inspection reveals that the actual bore begins about 5ft within so that the outer horse-shoe shaped mouth forms the attractive portal. Photo by David Ibbotson – date unknown

30. *The Railway Times*, 14 September 1832

31. Ibid, 26 September 1840.

32. Charles Hadfield, *The Canals of Yorkshire and North East England*, Vol.1, p.164.

33. *The Times*, 7 November 1839.

34. Ibid, 24 February 1840.

35. Tait and Butterworth, ibid.

36. *Herapath*, 13 October 1840.

Company had announced that to obviate the cost of building three bridges, only one would be built, the other two abandoned in favour of a diversion of the river (which would improve navigation), and the building of an embankment. Once again, the Navigation Company and a number of land owners were successful in preventing the railway company from proceeding, on the grounds that the railway plans had not been submitted for the Navigation Company to peruse. The *Wakefield Journal*, 19 April 1839, announced a 'Stoppage of Work near Wakefield', although it was still under the impression that three bridges were to built. The engineer's report given at a General Meeting held in Manchester on the 18 May 1839 referred to the bridge problem:

> The Kirkthorpe contract, as regards the embankment, is rapidly advancing. The other works on this contract cannot proceed more rapidly until the Act which is now before Parliament is obtained for making a diversion of the River Calder, which diversion will save the erection of two bridges, and will also straighten the navigation.

According to the Navigation Company's journal of accounts, dated 31 July 1839, a sum of £12,325 was paid by the railway company to the Navigation Company for the diversion of the river Calder at Broad Reach.

Despite this considerable sum of money, the Navigation Company, feeling threatened by the strength of the railway company, did everything possible to obstruct the progress of the railway. So did a small number of local land and property owners at Broad Reach namely the Lady William Gordon and the Earl of Westmorland. The matter really came to a head in March 1840 when the Navigation Company learned that a temporary bridge was to be built by the railway company as 'the most convenient and expeditions means of erecting a permanent one', but which might interfere with boats plying the river. Despite these attempts to impede the railway company, the bridge over the Calder at Broad Reach was erected. An engineers' report of 22 September 1839 had Stephenson and Gooch announcing that 'The contractor is now building the bridge over the crossing of the river, and he will use every exertion to complete it early so that the earthwork which is to form the embankment beyond the bridge may be led over it'.[30] Stephenson and Gooch's report twelve days earlier referred briefly to the Kirkthorpe contract in which 'rapid progress' was being made 'by continuous night and day work, coupled with favourable weather, by which means it will be completed a month earlier than was calculated upon'.[31] The bridge turned out to be a three-arch skewed stone structure, which led the railway on to the long embankment across land which had previously been occupied by a meander of the Calder. As it happened, the cut which had shortened the navigation from one side of the meander to the other was unnecessary. On 15 August 1839, the Navigation Company's new canal between Broad Reach and Stanley Ferry was inaugurated, representing one of the finest achievements of Hugh McKintosh, the general contractor.

A native of the area returning after a long absence would scarcely have recognised the man-made landscape of 1840, and had it not been for a shortage of money there might have been a canal-railway interchange at Broad Reach (a rare example of co-operation between the two companies) which would have added to the infrastructure even further. However, owing to the caution of both companies, the interchange never materialised.[32]

The railway company's solicitors were kept busy with yet another injunction between November 1839 and March 1840, this time involving the diversion of the Calder at Healey, about one mile west of Horbury. The Company had obtained an Act (the last of three which empowered it to divert the Calder) but not to interfere with the supply of water to Healey New Mill, a wool scribbling and cleaning business which relied heavily on water drawn off the river. This, it was claimed, the Company had done, 'the effect of which would be to give a new direction to the current and leave the plaintiff's mill entirely dry'.[33] To add insult to injury, an access road (Jacob's Road) to the mill had been altered so that it had become unsuitable for transporting packages of wool 'and was besides dangerous, being for a short distance parallel with the railroad and then descending spirally and passing under a low arch instead of being on a level as heretofore'.[34] After months of dispute a decision was reached in favour of the railway company which, it was stated, had acted as authorised and on which work had commenced as early as April 1838, long before the complaints made by the owner of Healey New Mill. On this occasion, the Calder & Hebble Navigation Company were not involved.

On top of all this, as if the Company had not endured enough complications, an incident took place at the eastern extremity of the line at the beginning of 1840. The *Wakefield Journal*, 4 January, related the story as follows:

On Tuesday, an accident occurred at Goose Hill, on the line of the Manchester and Leeds Railway. The workmen who were finishing the contracts, had not connected the rails when they finished work for the day. The consequence was the five o'clock train went off the 'rubbish line', and came into contact with the contractor's waggons, which, of course, sustained considerable damage, and this, with the consequent fright of the passengers, is, we believe, the extent of the mischief. The head servant of the contractor is in

custody to answer the charge of neglect in the room of the 'ganger', who has absconded.

Hugh McKintosh's feelings on the subject were not recorded!

Several stations were opened simultaneously on 5 October 1840, the day the line was opened between Normanton and Hebden Bridge: Elland, Brighouse, Cooper Bridge, Dewsbury, Horbury and Wakefield. Of these, only Brighouse and Cooper Bridge received a mention by Butterworth in his description of the line: Brighouse – 'one of the most important stations on the line, a tastefully constructed edifice, somewhat in the Chinese style. This is the nearest point on the railway, at present, to the large town of Bradford, which is seven miles distant, to the north'. Cooper Bridge was briefly described as 'the station for Huddersfield and adjacent places'.[35] *Herapath*, in its description of the opening of the line also referred to two of the stations, Wakefield and Dewsbury. Of the former – 'The station house is a neat and commodious brick building'; while Dewsbury deserved the following – 'The station house here is built of stone, and, like other stations on the line, it is neat but not very ornamental'.[36] Neatness without elaboration seemed to be the hallmark of the Manchester & Leeds structures.

The last leg of the M&L route lay between Wakefield and Goose Hill Junction, Normanton. This involved crossing the Calder at Broad Reach, east of Wakefield. The river in this low-lying, flat terrain is characterised by wide and sinuous meanders with abandoned river bends, making the ground wet and marshy. The canalised section forming the Aire & Calder Navigation began at Broad Reach, just north of the bridge. Much of the engineering work involved diverting the river to the east of the bridge and the construction of a high embankment to carry the railway over the low-lying flood plain. Photographed 31 March 1997 by the author

FOUR

The Summit Tunnel

Almost immediately after quitting Littleborough, the celebrated Vale of Todmorden commences. The railway, on its approach to the Summit Tunnel, is carried along by a cutting of nearly a hundred feet at its greatest depth. This extraordinary subterranean work, one of the triumphs of modern skill, presents, even at its mouth, a highly impressive appearance.[37]

So wrote Edwin Butterworth in 1842 in the year after the tunnel had been completed. He was very obviously impressed by the monumental civil engineering involved. Although Stephenson and Gooch played the chief role in the construction of the tunnel, the final accolade should be bestowed on the resident engineer, Barnard Dickinson, and the contractor, John Stephenson. Dickinson had been appointed assistant to Stephenson and Gooch with an annual salary of £400[38], and the work of sinking the shafts placed in the hands of the contractors, Evans & Copeland – their tender of £107,800 having been accepted on 27 December 1837.

Work began on sinking the shafts in January 1838. The Board Minutes of 20 August 1838 refer to the visit of several Directors on the 17th of that month, accompanied by the Chairman, James Wood, to the workings at Summit. Here, Mr Wood and others descended No.10 shaft, he having the pleasure of laying the first brick in the tunnel. At the surface, the construction of the railway had considerable impact on the surrounding hillsides of the Todmorden Valley. The

Manchester Guardian, 22 August 1838, described the scene as witnessed by one of its reporters:

On returning through the romantic Vale of Todmorden, preparations are in progress on an extensive scale; the lofty hills which hem in the canal, the river, and the road, leading in some places to no obvious footing for a railway, are at several points already deeply scooped out, the valuable stone they contain being laid in heaps, ready for further operations; while at the sides of some of them, large numbers of men are occupied in detaching still more ponderous portions of the stone. Temporary railways cross the turnpike road repeatedly, for the purpose of conveying what is won from the hill sides to the point where it will be put to the best use.

Somewhere amongst the heaps of stone and waggon-ways, a group of cottages was located, having been built for the purpose of accommodating workmen. Board Minutes of 22 October 1838 refer to twenty cottages to be let for the workmen who were employed on the tunnel by the recommendation of Gooch. Since many hundreds of men were employed, the cottages would hold but a few of them, and the implication is that the selected few were foremen, time-keepers and overseers. A much later report in *Herapath*, 2 January 1841, referred to seventy houses built by the Company 'for dwellings for the work people, who have also built for themselves about 100 huts on the Summit, above the tunnel'.

A comprehensive public reference to the tunnel appeared in *The Railway Times* on 24 March 1838, and involved a

37. Tait and Butterworth, *Views on the Manchester and Leeds Railway*, 1842.

38. M&L Board Minutes, 28 January 1838.

judicial inquiry into the loss of 18 acres of land which belonged to James Dearden Esq., Lord of the Manor, Rochdale, the land allegedly containing beneath the surface valuable 'mines and minerals'. The report of the inquiry makes fascinating reading, but the comments made by James Copeland, one of the contractors, under examination, furnish details of the progress which had at that time (16 March) been made:

> We have sunk eleven shafts which we have sunk to the following depths –
>
> | | | | |
> |---|---|---|---|
> | No.1 | 25½ yards | No.7 | 59 yards |
> | No.2 | 46½ yards | No.8 | 42 yards |
> | No.3 | 26 yards | No.9 | 42 yards |
> | No.4 | 36 yards | No.10 | 37 yards |
> | No.5 | 38½ yards | No.11 | 46 yards |
> | No.6 | 55 yards | | |

The compensation demanded by Dearden, for the minerals alone, amounted to £30,000! The Company was obliged to pay a total of £150, by the unanimous decision of the jury.

George Stephenson had to allay fears that the tunnel was being bored through treacherous rock. His report, of 24 March 1838, refuted any claims of dangerous geological conditions:

> The tunnel at the summit of the country may be considered the greater work upon the line; and I am happy in being able to confirm my former ideas as to the soundness of the material at this place for tunnelling through, as the whole of the shafts are sunk to a sufficient depth to prove beyond doubt that the material is of a firm and sound description.

Whishaw described the strata through which the tunnel passed as being 'through shales, rock, clays, bin, etc'.[39]

One year later and it appears that progress with the tunnel was beset with minor problems. Stephenson and Gooch's report, published in *The Railway Times*, 30 March 1839, sounded a note of dissatisfaction:

> The tunnel at the summit of the country is not being

proceeded with as rapidly as the contractors ought to do, and some changes must be immediately made as regards the number of men employed, and the general management of the work. If a sufficient number of men be employed, there can be no difficulty in completing the tunnel in the year 1840. The total length of the driftway is 3,080 yards of which 1,840 is completed, leaving 1,240 to be executed. The completion of the driftway is of very great importance not only for draining off the water, but it will give better admission of air. From the large size which it is being made, we shall be able, when it is finished, to commence tunnelling at a point immediately between the shafts, and thus increase the number of faces for the tunnel.

Board Minutes dated 21 January 1839 hinted at the core of the problem, that of James Copeland who was 'experiencing some pecuniary difficulties'. By 8 March, Robert Gill, the Managing Director, recommended that the Evans & Copeland contract should be cancelled and re-let to other contractors. Two such contractors presented their tenders: Harding & Cropper, and John Stephenson (no relation to George). The latter contractor was hired to continue where

The western portal of Summit Tunnel is framed within the elliptical arch and masonry invert of the 55yd long Summit West Tunnel. This short brick-arch tunnel carried the railway beneath the Littleborough to Todmorden turnpike and though of minor importance compared to its nearby neighbour, boasts the only known M&L crest which is carved in the pediment above the tunnel mouth. Photographed 29 May 1997 by the author

39. Francis Whishaw, *The Railways of Great Britain and Ireland*, 1842.

The eastern portal of Summit Tunnel is prosaic in comparison to the embellished western end. This view has been snatched by the cameraman during a brief interval in the passage of trains, and taken from within the short Summit East Tunnel. Although one continuous tunnel with different profiles, the apparent break at this point is due to an elliptical shaft (The Great Shaft) which allows the penetration of daylight enough to photograph the place in which permanent-way men have erected cabins

Below: The 41yd long stretch of Summit East Tunnel looked like this in early BR days. The view will have not changed much since M&L trains reached daylight after their passage through Summit Tunnel, except for the modern track, ballast, and other ephemeral man-made features. Hidden from view is the tunnel lining which was renewed in 1909/10

Photos J.A. Peden Collection

Evans & Copeland had left off, the termination of their work incurring a penalty of £3,000. *The Railway Times*, 11 May 1839, received news of the change and briefly stated that 'This great undertaking has been relinquished by Messrs Evans & Copeland. The Company have appointed John Stephenson Esq. as their successor to work the tunnel'.

This was not the end of the matter, however. Board Minutes of the 20 and 26 September 1839 reveal that the newly-appointed contractor, after a few months, was not happy with the details of the contract. Gooch had recommended that £3,500 be paid on the account of John Stephenson, who in turn, 'most unexpectedly made a further request that the Company should pay him an additional £5 per lineal yard on

the work yet to be done at the Summit Tunnel'. Stephenson was questioned on his reasons for applying for the advance of £5 per lineal yard, and replied that he was losing money on the contract, mainly from the increase in the cost of mining of £3 per yard, and from a doubling of expenses. Having already lost £3,000, Stephenson felt that to continue would lead him to ruin. The Board saw fit to retain his services, with an advance of £10,000 and the payment of a bonus of £5,000 if the contract was completed in the specified time.

A more optimistic tone is evident in the Engineer's Report which appeared in *The Railway Times*, 14 September 1839: 'The present rate of progress is about 140 yards per month', but this was a rate not realistically expected to continue. Yet, a series of notes appearing in the Board Minutes revealed that the Company's exhortation for the contractor to press ahead were successful: '7th November 1839 – 168 yards of tunnelling done during the month of October, a decided improvement. 5th December 1839 – progress satisfactory with 156 yards done in November. 6th February 1840 – 141 lineal yards and 16 yards of driftway during January. 23rd April 1840 – 163 yards of tunnelling and 18 yards of drift-way during March. On the whole, going satisfactorily, and Mr Gooch still expects to complete it in November next. 7th May 1840 – 105 yards done during the month. Progress not so satisfactory last month in consequence of a turn-out of bricklayers, but improving now ... 5th November 1840 – 40 yards during October; 31 yards remaining on 1st November. Bonus for October, £143 13s 4d'. A bonus scheme had been introduced by Gooch during June 1840 in order to enhance the rate of progress. This was the final report given concerning the tunnel, its completion therefore having been made probably in early December.

Accidents had happened far too often. A very illuminating letter was sent to the editor of *The Railway Times* from J.D. Barry at the Associated Contractors' offices in Manchester. The letter was in response to press reports of a number of accidents which had occurred during construction of the tunnel so far. The full missive appeared in the journal on 5 October 1839 and is quoted here in its entirety since it

The western portal of Summit Tunnel as seen today from the Littleborough to Todmorden road. Tait's view (see page 41) exaggerates the rock terrain above the mouth, and from this view it is easy to see why. The craggy hillock is entirely natural whereas the sides of the approach cutting are man-made, resulting from blasting of the rock with gunpowder. J.A. Peden Collection

shows how the men were treated by the considerate attitude of the contractor:

Very exaggerated statements of the number of fatal accidents on this work are in circulation, and have obtained a certain degree of authority by having appeared in your journal. Although the number is not thirty, as has been stated, it is unhappily very considerable. From the 19th February 1838, the date of the last casualty, to the 11th September last, a period of 19 months, the total fatal accidents was 16. The names of the sufferers, and the circumstances of each casualty are now before me, obtained from the record I kept at the works. In the great majority of cases, I find the accident attributable to the carelessness or misconduct of the men themselves; and the remainder to arise from causes, more or less, inseparable from the construction of works of the nature and magnitude of this stupendous tunnel. In one case only – that of the poor miner, Roger Warrin, who was killed by a fragment of rock at distance of 60 yards from the explosion – does it appear that the sufferers were married . . . To all to whom the respected contractor Mr John Stephenson is known, it is unnecessary to say that every precaution, which judgement and great experience in this description of work can suggest to

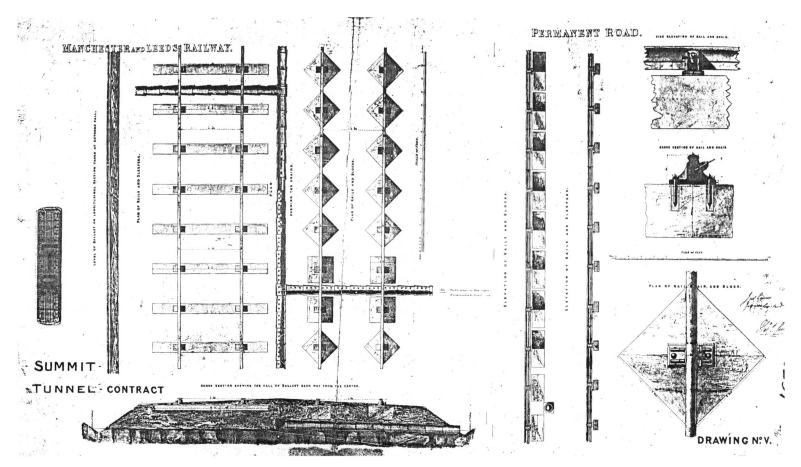

Summit Tunnel Contract –
Permanent Way.

Two methods of laying the
track are shown – on timber
sleepers and on stone blocks.
The latter weighed ¼ ton each
and were set diagonally at
3ft centres to counteract the
horizontal thrust of trains
passing over them.

The method of drainage,
canting of the rails, and the
method of rail-chair fixing also
appear on the drawing

guard against accidents, the humanity to alleviate them
when they do occur, is strictly attended to on his part.
To those men who do not know him it may be as well
to state that all the tackle and gearing are all of the best
description and periodically inspected as to their
sufficiency by his principal agents; that the regulations
for carrying on the works, descending the pits, etc, are
well-calculated to guard against accidents; that a
building has been erected for an hospital and a surgeon
paid £20 a month for his attention on the works; and
that every man employed is required to contribute one
shilling per fortnight to a fund for the relief of sufferers
by casualties who are allowed ten shillings a week until

able to resume their employment. In case of death, the
contribution is 6d extra for the wife and family of the
deceased after defraying the funeral expenses. Nor is
Mr Stephenson less solicitous about the spiritual wants
of his men than careful for their temporal necessities.
He prefers in the first instance, and promotes
afterwards, steady, sober, moral men rather than more
experienced and better workmen who are drunken and
dissolute; and has given £30 towards the erection of a
place of worship for the men in encouragement of the
laudable desire expressed by some of them to subscribe
for that purpose.

1st October 1839.

Despite this generous welfare towards the men, labour trouble flared up from time to time. The *Manchester Guardian*, 28 March 1840, related the news of sixteen labourers who were employed at the tunnel and who were charged with intimidating other workmen 'by threats from following their employment'. The affair reached the magistrates' court:

> Mr Stephenson, railway contractor, stated that the defendants had seriously annoyed 32 labourers who had lately arrived from North Shields and who were engaged for six months at 5s per day. On Saturday last, the old hands assembled in large numbers and attempted to persuade the rival operatives to quit their work at once.

In this the intimidation appeared to be successful as the new men were few in number ready to begin work on Monday morning, the rest having been cajoled away from work by a promise of 35 shillings each if they stayed away from work. The ruse was discovered by John Stephenson, and was perceived as having trade-union undertones. The Rochdale magistrates, Royds and Chadwick, standing no nonsense, committed six of the 'conspirators' to three months hard labour.

With the tunnel almost completed, (the last brick was laid by Barnard Dickinson on 9 December 1840), great expectations were about as to the opening of the line throughout. Gooch had inspected the tunnel by walking through it in mid November, and was confident that the line would be opened by 21 December. The Board of Trade were given notice of the intended opening on that date. Thus the final obstacle to the through

communication seemed imminent. At the eleventh hour, George Stephenson, Gooch, and their assistant, Dickinson, were confronted with an unforeseen setback. The *Manchester Guardian* of 19 December, revealed the problem:

> Some excitement was caused upon the Manchester Exchange on Thursday last by a report to the effect that a portion of the Summit Tunnel on the Manchester and Leeds Railway, extending about 50 yards in length, had fallen in. We find, however, upon inquiry from the offices of the Company, that, though there has been a partial failure of a portion of the tunnel, it is by no means of so serious a character as was first represents. It appears that in a piece of soft ground between Shafts No.2 and No.3, the inverted arch (which forms the bottom of the tunnel), has been pushed upwards by the pressure of the earth for a distance of 80 yards, but the side walls and roof remain perfectly uninjured. We believe it is the opinion of the engineer that the defective portion of the arch will have to be removed, which will probably occupy four or five weeks, and in that case will retard the general opening of the line for traffic.

The Board Minutes repeatedly refer to the invert problem throughout the December of 1840. On 4 December, for instance, it was reported that stretchers had been put in as a precautionary measure to keep the walls intact in case the invert should move upwards still further. Gooch considered that all the repairs necessary were attributable to the defective invert, and recommended that a stronger

Two examples of the original Summit Tunnel shaft-heads which mark the alignment of the tunnel on the moorland surface. No.3 is a squat version, the exterior constructed of dressed stone, while No.6, rising some 20ft, has been built of brickwork with a thin stone capping. All the shafts of the tunnel were relined with brickwork between 1901 and 1907. Author

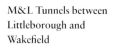

M&L Tunnels between Littleborough and Wakefield

Littlebrough Station
Summit West 55 yards
Summit 2,885 yards
Summit East 41 yards
Deanroyd 70 yards
Winterbutlee 306 yards
Walsden Station
Todmorden Station
Millwood 225 yards
Castle Hill 194 yards
Horsfall 274 yards
Eastwood Station
Weasel Hall 109 yards
Hebden Bridge Station
Sowerby Bridge 657 yards
Sowerby Bridge Station
Elland 420 yards
Elland Station
Horbury Station
Horbury 128 yards
Wakefield Station

invert should be constructed extending beyond the fractured part. In his opinion, no change of any consequence had occurred in the side walls during the last few days, and he hoped that everything would be finished in February.

On 21 December, Stephenson and Gooch felt obliged to forward a letter of explanation to the Directors who were waiting, with some impatience, to open the tunnel. It was a letter which attempted to engender confidence and at the same time assuage anxiety felt by the Directors as to the sturdiness of the tunnel.

> We beg to inform you that we have closely inspected the fractured part of the invert in the Summit Tunnel between No.2 and 3 shafts, which has been referred to in Mr Dickinson's last reports. About 80 yards in length shows symptoms of weakness but the defect has been discovered before any movement has taken place to affect the stability of the Arching and Side Walls, which are in a sound and perfect state, and we seen no reason whatever to apprehend that any further derangement in them will occur. The tunnel at this part passes through an extensive fault in the strata commencing near to No.3 shaft and extending about 120 yards towards No.2. The material is very much dislocated, of an uncertain and variable character, and the bottom being soft has a strong tendency to rise, from the superincumbent weight on the invert on the [undecipherable]. This has thrown a greater weight on the invert than we expected which, however, will be sufficiently strengthened by being constructed of stone and increased in thickness, and there is no doubt that by the adoption of this plan, the Tunnel will be made perfectly secure. This operation cannot be effected in less than six weeks but may possibly occupy two months – we should recommend therefore that the line will be opened up to the East of the Tunnel as early as practicable, and so we expect to have both lines of Rails from Hebden Bridge to this point laid by the middle of this week it may be opened during the present year. You may be assured that no time will be lost in making the Tunnel complete.

Board Minutes for 25 January and 8 February 1841 indicate the care taken by Gooch to ensure the complete safety of the tunnel. On the 25th, it was reported that 60 yards of invert had been repaired, and that a further 60 yards still required attention. On the 8th, Gooch reported that unlike the Charlestown Tunnel, the Summit Tunnel could not move as it had been driven through competent rock with the exception of 250 yards at the eastern end (where the uplifted invert was located) which runs through rock debris. The tunnel had not moved in the twelve months since its completion, and the date was set for public opening on the 1 March 1841.

Herapath, 2 January 1841, touched upon interesting aspects of the tunnel, of which the following is a brief resume. The tunnel had taken two years and four months to construct and had employed between 800 and 1,200 men, 120 to 140 horses, and 13 stationary engines which were equivalent to 202 horse power. Twenty-three million bricks were used to line the tunnel, and a large quantity of ashlar stones, and pierre-pointing requiring 8,000 tons of Roman cement instead of ordinary mortar. At 2,869 yards (sic) (the accepted length today is taken at 2,885 yards) it was, on completion, longer than the Kilsby Tunnel on the London & Birmingham Railway by 417 yards. John Marshall has the total cost of the Summit Tunnel as £251,000.[40] The distinction of being the longest tunnel was ephemeral; by 1845, the Woodhead Tunnel had surpassed it at 5,302 yards. In a communication to the Directors, dated 27 February 1841, Gooch had the pleasure to report, 'that the works on the portion of your line, not yet opened, and which were unfinished at the date of Sir F. Smith's inspection, are completed, including both lines of railway; and I have no hesitation in stating that it may be travelled in perfect safety by the public'.

In a terse statement in the Board Minutes, dated 22 March 1841, Mr Dickinson reported the tunnel 'to be laid at rest' – a telling remark; it was as if the dreaded ghost of unpredictable tunnel failure had at last been exorcised.

40. John Marshall, *The Lancashire & Yorkshire Railway*, Vol.1., p.43.

VIEWS

ON THE

MANCHESTER

and

LEEDS

RAILWAY

•

Drawn from Nature
and on Stone by

A.F. TAIT

A.F. Tait
– a short biography

THE illustrations in this supplement have been selected out of a total of nineteen lithographs which appeared in 'Views on the Manchester and Leeds Railway', published in 1845 in collaboration with Edwin Butterworth who furnished a 'descriptive history' of the line.

Arthur Fitzwilliam Tait was born on 5 August 1819 at Livesey Hall, near Liverpool, the son of a Manchester businessman. As a child he attended a county school in Lancashire, and at the age of twelve went to work in Agnew's Repository of the Arts where he was exposed to the art of Edwin Landseer and J.F. Herring, and was encouraged to try his hand at lithography. In the 1830s and 1840s lithographs were in great demand in England. However, he discovered that as a young adult, finding work to earn a living was very difficult, and had to resort to drawing churches to this end, a task which must have been irksome to a convinced atheist. The successful opening of the Manchester & Leeds Railway prompted him to fashion a set of lithographs which depicted scenes along the line. According to Jack Simmons, 'Their detail is sharp, and Tait showed a careful observation of some of the railway's civil engineering works, for example, the Gauxholme viaduct, as well as what was most congenial to him, the railway's passage through the open landscape'.

Tait also turned his attention to a set of lithographs showing aspects of the north-western division of the London & North Western Railway. These were never completed or published, but they can be seen at the National Railway Museum at York.

In 1850 Tait emigrated to America where he found success as an artist, producing over 1,700 paintings of birds, animals and sportsmen during his life time. He died at the age of 86 at Yonkers, New York, on 28 April 1905. It is significant that he never returned to England.

OVERLEAF:
'Amidst piles of towering shapeless crags whose face and form have been altered by the labours of man, and the blasting of gunpowder, rises a fine massive arch of masonry of admirable workmanship, and elegant proportions'. Butterworth was obviously impressed by the location of the western portal of the Summit Tunnel, and although Tait exaggerated the height of the rocky eminence above, today's visitor also finds the spot awe-inspiring when seen from the road which skirts the deep approach cutting

The last section of the Liverpool & Manchester Railway before the end-on junction with the M&L was effected by means of two iron bridges immediately to the west of Victoria Station. Far right is the 120ft span across the river Irwell; next to it is the Great Ducie Street bridge forming a span of 83ft. Both bridges were erected by the Liverpool Company. A train can be seen about to cross the road bridge *en route* to Victoria Station. Beyond the road bridge there is a glimpse of the Palatine Hotel, a prominent edifice described by Butterworth as 'a handsome structure' which overlooked Hunt's Bank. The uppermost part of the tower of Manchester Cathedral peeps above the ornamental iron parapet

The Victoria Station house opened on 1 January 1844, and was described by the *Manchester Guardian* as possessing two fronts, 'the north to the railway and the south to the carriage way on the approach, and facing also the back of Cheetham's College'. Designed in the Roman Doric Style, the station house was a single-storey building, measuring about 266ft by 36ft, and constructed out of parr-point, a much-used stone quarried in the Brighouse area. The western end of the building (far distant) was occupied by the L&M Company, the other half used by the M&L. The whole comprised public utilities, stationmaster's residence, offices, and refreshment rooms

Described as being larger than Derby Station, Victoria Station encompassed turntables, sidings, and arrival/departure platforms for use by both companies. The iron-roofed and partially-glazed train shed was erected so as to form three compartments, the central one shown here being 59ft 6in. wide. The overall area of the train-shed roofing covered almost 80,000 sq. ft. During the day there was adequate light provided by the natural daylight through the skylights: by night, Hall's flat-flame gas burners furnished sufficient illumination. The first and second-class refreshment room at the northern end of the station house is marked by the bay window overlooking the platform. Third-class passengers had to make do with refreshments served in a basement room, out of sight of the better-class clientele

Butterworth confined his comments about Rochdale Station to noting that it was 'a small but yet commodious and neat edifice, apparently well-adapted for the accommodation of passengers'. As an ancient and flourishing textile town Rochdale was the most important settlement through which the main line ran on the north side of Manchester. The view shows the Up-platform shelter to the right, and the main buildings which were on the town-centre side (this being about half a mile away) on the left. In the distance stands Rochdale engine shed complete with pump-house chimney.

Note the locomotive standing on the Down line and taking water from a water crane

The view looking west from elevated ground between the Pennines and the Rossendale Hills embraces
the uneven plain of the Roch Valley north of Rochdale. In this scene it is possible to trace the line of the railway
as it takes a sweeping curve via Littleborough (marked by the church spire), whereupon it is lost on the approach
to Rochdale (marked by the forest of mill and factory chimneys). The train is making its way towards the
Tunnel, the line running almost parallel with the Rochdale Canal which avoids the need of a tunnel
throughout its entire length

The cast-iron bridge over the Rochdale Canal was described by Butterworth as 'a costly and beautiful structure . . . supported at the angles by handsome castellated abutments of solid masonry, and yet possessing a most graceful appearance'. Viewed from the canal towpath, or the nearby main road, the bridge is still an arresting sight

Once located half in Lancashire and half in Yorkshire, Todmorden is said to have derived its name
from being 'the todlike, or deeply shaded mere of the dene or valley'. The Lancashire river Calder flows
through the town, its deep valley forcing the railway to maintain height and steady gradient by means of a
'noble viaduct of nine stately arches of free stone'. In this view we see the north-eastern aspect of the viaduct
as a train approaches the town's station. Note the levee separating the meandering Calder from the
cart track, and the jumble of railway-contractor's plant alongside

A view of Todmorden and the viaduct as seen from the north. This bucolic scene belies the fact that in the town,
and also around it, the textile industry with its associated manufacturing, flourished in stone mills and workshops.
The passage of the railway through the town was a boon to local manufacturers such as the Fielden Family
which, in 1846, consumed more raw cotton than any other firm in the country.

Butterworth painted a rosy picture of life in Todmorden when he alluded to the vale 'studded with cheerful
inhabitants'. During the lean 1840s the vicissitudes of the textile trade and the long hours of labour would have ensured
that impoverished families found it hard to be cheerful

Work appears to be continuing at the eastern end of the bridge which spanned the Rochdale Canal when Tait fashioned
this sketch. The cast-iron bridge was supported on four masonry abutments and was linked integrally with Whiteley's Viaduct
to the west. According to a map dated 9 August 1839 showing the disposition of the bridge, 'The angle of skew and dimensions
of the Bridge are the same as at the Second Canal crossing at Gauxholme'. Assuming Tait to have made an accurate
representation, the tall chimney on the Down side, and the nearby building on the Up side, would suggest that this
was the location of a pump house for watering purposes. It is worth mentioning that the constricted nature
of the Todmorden Valley forced the three modes of transport to vie for space

The Todmorden Valley through which the railway ran could be seen to advantage from the elevated ground
above Mytholm Church to the west of Hebden Bridge. The centre-piece of the scene is the railway bridge over
the Rochdale Canal and Whiteley's Viaduct spanning the Rochdale to Sowerby Bridge road, both dwarfed
by fold upon fold of steep slopes and the lofty ground above

Hebden Bridge Station, a view looking east towards Sowerby Bridge. Immediately to the left is the
winding river Calder, and to its left the Rochdale Canal. In order to reach the station from the town, it was
necessary to cross both the canal and the river – the two bridges carrying the approach road can be
clearly seen. The main station building was located on the Down side nearest to the town centre.
A single-road goods shed or engine shed was served by a trailing connection on the Up line.
A Stephenson 2-2-2 runs light engine to the west of the station

'One of the most important stations on the line, a tastefully constructed edifice, somewhat in the Chinese style' is how Butterworth described Brighouse Station. This was located on the southern fringes of the town, most of the town occupying land which sloped upward from the river Calder. The view shows the elegant station buildings which were positioned on the Down side closest to the town centre. The scene depicts one of some activity as men push and ride a platelayer's wagon alongside the low-level platform, whilst three men direct proceedings with a horse and cart in attendance.

Note the canopy over the lengthy Down platform and the water crane positioned behind the fence.

The building on the far left could be yet another pump house

A bevy of bonneted ladies with children sit at the top of the cutting which existed to the east of Wakefield Station.
Wakefield Station was the last to serve the M&L before the Company's line merged with the North Midland Railway
at Goose Hill Junction. The station occupied a Down-side site, once again being nearest to the town centre, in an area known
as Kirkgate. The railway approached the station from the west over the sixteen-arched Wakefield Viaduct and left the station
via a cutting which merited some recognition; according to Butterworth: 'On quitting Wakefield the railway enters
a deep cutting, where coal strata may be distinctly traced'. Far right is the 288ft high spire of
All Saints Parish Church (now Wakefield Cathedral), a prominent landmark

Opened on 1 July 1840 by the NMR, Normanton Station was soon to become a major junction serving not only
its parent company but also the M&L, and the Y&NM Railways. Butterworth considered that the station possessed 'neat
offices, commodious refreshment rooms, and a splendid hotel' all built for the convenience of passengers and visitors. From the
station it was possible to take the train to 'almost every part of the kingdom'. The amenity was particularly noted for its
refreshment facilities and hotel, both interconnected with the station by means of covered footbridges. Normanton lay
in the heart of coal-mining country and shared in this primary industry as it developed during the rest of the century

FIVE

Grand Openings and Subsequent Events

Captain Laws laid on the table . . . a number of books and forms which he had prepared for the working of the line. Also an advertisement announcing to the public that the Railway will open for the conveyance of Passengers on Thursday the 4th July next.

COMMITTEE OF MANAGEMENT MEETING, 2 JUNE 1839.

MAY 31 1839 was a special day. Directors, shareholders and their friends boarded three carriages (two second class and one third class) at the temporary station, St George's Fields, Manchester, for the first train journey to the entrance of the Summit Tunnel. The short train set off at 10.50 a.m, but had to be drawn by horses owing to the absence of the L&M Company's locomotive, *Lancaster* which had been planned to haul them on the first leg of the journey. About 4½ miles from the terminus, the permanent single line ended and it was necessary for the party of sixty gentlemen to alight and walk ¾ mile to a second train waiting for them on the next set of rails. Locomotive No.212, *Stephenson*, drew the train forward, attaining a speed of 30 miles an hour, and arrived at the temporary Rochdale Station at 12.35 p.m. Here, the train halted and the engine was detached from the carriages for the purpose of taking water, 'which was effected by means of a fire engine, belonging to the Rochdale police, pumping from a brook over which the railway passes'.[41] After a period of twenty minutes, the train set off again and arrived at the Summit Tunnel at 1.30 p.m. The party gave the tunnel a general inspection, whereupon, feeling satisfied by what they had

seen, they retired for luncheon which was served in the third class carriage. At 3 p.m, the return journey commenced amidst the cheers of spectators who had gathered at the place. The *Lancaster* locomotive now awaited their arrival at Moston and conveyed the party back to Manchester. The day had been trouble-free, and the trip regarded as a 'successful experiment'.

This event was a precursor of the grand opening of the line between Manchester and the Summit Tunnel which took place on Wednesday, 3 July 1839. Such was the occasion that not only were the Directors and shareholders of the Company involved, but those of other railway companies (not least the L&M with whom the M&L needed good relations). There too were the officers of Manchester-based regiments, magistrates of local authorities, and a host of ladies and gentlemen. All were accommodated in two trains of eleven carriages each, the first drawn by the locomotives *Stephenson* and *Kenyon*, the second by *Stanley* and *Lancaster*. *The Railway Times*, in its 13 July edition, gave an abridged account which had been taken from the *Manchester Guardian*: 'The carriages were decorated for the occasion with a number of small flags and banners, on most of which were inscribed some loyal sentiments as "Queen Victoria – God bless her!", "Long live the Queen", and "Peace and Concord". The first train set off at 12.22 p.m. and was followed ten minutes later by the second. Of the first train,

Mills Hill station, distance 5½ miles from Manchester, was reached in 22 minutes before one o'clock . . . As the train approached the station, the

41. *The Railway Times*, 8 June 1839.

conductor's bugle commenced playing 'God Save the Queen', the band of the 86th took up the strain of the National Anthem, and the train reached the station amidst the cheers of a concourse of people, drawn to this point both from Oldham and Middleton.

Unfortunately, the steady progress of the first train out of Manchester came to an unexpected halt as it climbed the 1 in 130 gradient on the approach to Blue Pits (Castleton). *Kenyon* lost power and expired, leaving *Stephenson* with the impossible task of hauling the stricken engine and eleven carriages. *Kenyon's* water supply pump was found on inspection to be clogged with mud. At this juncture, the party of travellers alighted (with the exception of the ladies) in order to lighten the load, so that *Lancaster* could move forward again to the strain of the conductor's bugle playing 'Oh, dear, what can the matter be?' By this time, the second train had caught up and was coupled up to the rear of the first, and, 'with the *Stephenson* engine at the head of the whole, the train started again on its way, after a delay of nearly three quarters of an hour, about seventeen minutes after one o'clock'.

On arriving at Rochdale, it was observed that, 'The station-house here is quite finished, except for the interior fittings, about which we noticed workmen busily employed. On the roof were hoisted a number of flags in honour of the day and others were displayed from various buildings on or near the line.' The disgraced *Kenyon* was shunted into a siding for immediate repairs. The other locomotives took on coke and water, 'the latter being supplied by a canvas hose from a cast-iron pump, the arm of which, by means of its axis, and balance weight, was swung round so as to extend over the rails to the back of the tender'. At 1.58 p.m. the long train of three locomotives and twenty-two carriages passed through Littleborough, all aboard noticing 'with no little satisfaction two long ranges of sideboards loaded with all the materials of a substantial collation', and much to their consternation, the train did not stop, but proceeded almost to the entrance of the Summit Tunnel, where the passengers detrained. Some ventured into the tunnel, strolling as far as the first shaft, whilst

others walked back towards Littleborough, no doubt attracted by the victuals there.

At 3 p.m. the official cold collation began, the 500 or so guests of the M&L Company ensconced in the unfinished station-house. The *Manchester Courier*, 6 July 1839, gave its own account of the proceedings, commenting that, 'The building . . . is as yet only roofed on one side, but to guard against the effects of weather, in case it had proved adverse, a canvas covering was extended over the rafters on the other side. The ends of the building which are quite open, were also similarly protected'. Meanwhile, the engines and carriages had returned to Rochdale where the former were supplied with coke and water for the return journey. *Kenyon's* pump had now been cleared of the choking mud and was able to join the two trains for the journey back to Manchester. The first and second arrived back at the terminus at 5.27 p.m. and 6.20 p.m. respectively. The line, thus being officially opened by this event, was available for public use the following day. A timetable appeared in *The Railway Times* on 27 July, advertising that there would be four morning and four afternoon trains in both directions, the journey time from Manchester to Littleborough being 45 minutes. The costs borne by the travelling public depended on the distance travelled, and the class of vehicle used:

Manchester to Rochdale			Mills Hill to Littleborough		
1st	2nd	3rd	1st	2nd	3rd
3/-	2/-	1/-	3/-	2/-	1/-

For those who wished to travel to Todmorden or Oldham, it was necessary to travel by road: *The Railway Times*, 20 July 1839, gave the details of how this could be done:

From this station, the present terminus of the line, passengers going forward to Yorkshire are to be conveyed by Messrs Lacy and Allen's coaches, which are to wait at this point the arrival of the various trains . . . At Mills Hill, omnibuses to and from Oldham and Middleton will wait and meet the trains, until the Oldham Branch of the railway is opened.

Earlier, at a meeting on 7 May, Captain Laws had presented a proposal from Ramsbottom & Wharton to run six omnibuses to and from Oldham to Mills Hill Station 'as often as the Company pleased, the distance to Oldham being 2½ miles exclusive of going round the town'. The proposal was refused.[42]

The partial opening was an immediate success. The *Manchester Guardian*, 21 August 1839, announced that

> The business on this railway continues very rapidly to increase. Last week, notwithstanding the disturbed state of the neighbourhood, it kept up; and this week is has taken a surprising start: the number of passengers conveyed on Monday having been no fewer than 4,365, whilst yesterday they reached 4,704; total for two days, 9,629.

A letter sent to the editor of *The Railway Times* on 21 August from the Superintendent's office, Hunt's Bank, spoke of the *Stephenson* engine which had been in service between Manchester and Littleborough: on the run between Manchester and Blue Pits (Castleton), a distance of just over seven miles, and over a gradient of 1 in 150 from Mills Hill.

> This engine took up a train of 694 passengers, besides guards, freepersons, enginemen, etc, in 25 minutes – five of which she stopped at the Mills Hill station – having to regain her speed on this steep gradient, which she did with great ease, going the whole distance at an average of 22 miles per hour.

The *Stephenson* was a product of Messrs R. Stephenson and Co., of Newcastle-upon-Tyne. It was a six-wheeled engine with 14-inch cylinders and an 18-inch stroke. The sight of this engine, hauling a rake of carriages up the Mills Hill Embankment, must have been an exhilerating experience.

The year 1839 closed with a major collision on the approach to Rochdale. A new engine from the works of Messrs Peel, Williams & Peel, Manchester, was set on the rails at the Manchester terminus, to carry luggage on an experimental trip to the Summit Tunnel. The train left at 9 a.m. with a gross load of 47 tons, and reached a speed of 30mph on the run up to Rochdale. The *Manchester Courier*, 21 December, having ascertained the correct details, gave a full account of the mishap:

> The directors have very properly adopted an excellent rule when any unusual train or engine is about to run on the line, namely, the affixing of a board at the back of the preceding train on which is printed in very large letters ENGINE FOLLOWING or TRAIN FOLLOWING . . . thus giving ample notice to all parties who may be engaged on the line to be on the look-out.

The rule was, for some reason, neglected on the Monday evening of 19 December. The previous train to leave the Manchester station did not bear such a board and the driver of the special luggage train was aware of this. As his train rushed on towards Rochdale, the driver made use of the whistle, 'for a long period', and when 160 yards from the station, he noticed a person waving his hand frantically (not a flag, which was the usual method) thereby giving warning of danger. The train slowed to 10mph by dint of drastic measures. 'The engine was backed by using the reversing gear, and when the whole power of the steam applied in an opposing direction, the double breaking being also put into action at the same time.' By now, the driver had discerned a waggon standing on the line in front of him, the line on this stretch

The M&L thought it appropriate to erect a brick engine shed close to their station at Blue Pits (later Castleton), two miles south of Rochdale. The branch line to Heywood was opened on 15 April 1841: this branched off the main line immediately to the south of Blue Pits Station, so forming one of the first junctions on the M&L railway. Whether this prompted the Company to erect this modest shed is open to question. When this photograph was taken on 31 March 1972 the building had come to the end of its life, having served as a goods shed for many years. Tom Wray

42. PRO RAIL 343/485.

being on a curve, the weather hazy, if not foggy. The collision was unavoidable. The waggon was destroyed, and the *Manchester* on its maiden run, receiving much damage, was derailed, 'and was within two feet of going over the side of a bridge'. The driver and a Peel, Williams & Peel foreman remained on the footplate and escaped without injury, whilst the fireman and another man jumped off before the impact. The *Manchester* was a six-wheeled engine which saved her from falling on her side as would a four-wheeled engine. Excitement indeed at the close of the year, only a few days before Christmas.

As we have seen, trial or experimental trips along a new section of line was a prerequisite to opening for public use. Such a trip was also performed on the eastern section as a means of ensuring the competence and safety of the newly-completed line. On 15 August 1840, the *Manchester Guardian* informed its readers that

On Saturday last an experimental trip was made on part of the unopened line of this railway for the

distance of sixteen miles commencing at Hebden Bridge and continuing to Bradley Wood, near Mirfield . . . At one o'clock pm a train of ten carriages drawn by eight horses decorated with evergreens and rosettes of the gayest description, started from the former place, carrying nearly 100 individuals . . . and accompanied by two bands of music which greatly livened the proceedings of the day.

Crowds of people watched the event, and at Brighouse, a 'splendid cold collation was laid out on two very long tables in the open air'. The day was blessed with fine, bright weather which further enhanced an occasion of 'great hilarity', which took place without a single mishap or accident.

The second partial opening of the line west of Normanton to Hebden Bridge formed a distance of 27 miles out of a total of 58, and was opened with great ceremony 'for the conveyance of passengers' on 5 October 1840. The first train to run the full distance started from Leeds at 7.53 a.m. from a new station at Hunslet Lane. An undisclosed and apparently

Todmorden station, from a point overlooking the station in a south-easterly direction. This was the full extent of the station in LYR days, circa 1900. A radial-tank engine is engaged in a spot of shunting at the station; it is occupying the Up line at the Rochdale end of the station. The coal yard is well-stocked with a variety of mineral waggons, many privately owned by colliery companies. Careful observation shows the covered footbridge which linked the station to the Queen's Hotel, the curve of the line eastwards over the Todmorden Viaduct, and Todmorden East signal box beyond the viaduct. LYRS Collection

inadequate number of carriages belonging to the North Midland Company were drawn by a single locomotive loaned by the same. (This was an expedient borne out of an agreement between the two companies to apply until the M&L could provide its own rolling stock on completion of the Summit Tunnel). *The Railway Times*, 17 October 1840, drawing its information and enthusiasm from the *Leeds Mercury*, gave a full and lucid description of the occasion. 'The ten miles to Normanton were travelled in twenty-four minutes. At this place, a little to the north of the junction of the North Midland and the Manchester & Leeds, the foundations are laying for a station for the latter company.' Wakefield was passed through without inviting comment but at Thornhill (the station which served Dewsbury): 'A great number of persons had collected to witness the arrival of the train, and two omnibuses were standing, one of which, with four horses gaily caparisoned, is intended to run from the station to Dewsbury'. At Thornhill, the train was met by another which had travelled from Hebden Bridge, 'piloted by Mr Gooch, the Engineer, who quitted it at this point, and returned with the Leeds train to Hebden Bridge'. Again at Brighouse, crowds of people, many of whom had paid for the privilege of travelling on the train 'could not be accommodated in the carriages', the overflow mounting the carriage roofs to sit 'not in a safe position'. Despite being much overburdened, the train continued its pioneering journey westward to Hebden Bridge. Let *The Railway Times* take up the story again:

> At exactly half-past ten, having crossed the Blackstone edge turnpike road and the Ripponden stream (river Ryburn) by a handsome viaduct of five arches . . . we drew up at Sowerby Bridge station 32 miles from Leeds and 28 from Manchester. Here the crowd of people was so great, and the rush of those who had taken places to the carriages so alarming, that, after a brief stay of four minutes, it was thought absolutely necessary to move on. There being no room in the carriages, the adventurous travellers mounted the tops of the carriages, where already as many persons were

sitting as could be accommodated in that position; but those who could not sit stood upright, until the whole of the carriages were covered with a crowd of standers, and in that fearful position did they remain all the way to Hebden Bridge, stooping down as they passed under the tunnel and the numerous bridges on the line, and then rising and cheering like a crew of sailors to the astonished spectators.

An amusing incident occurred as the train drew away from Sowerby Bridge Station. The luggage of three 'revising barristers', Lutwidge, Cleasby and Doyle (sounding like characters out of a Dickens novel), who had travelled from Wakefield, bound for Halifax, had detrained amongst the seething mass at the station, only to find that their luggage had remained on the train as it hastily moved out of the station. This led to a comical scene:

> The barristers, alarmed at the prospect of losing their paraphernalia, ran after the train calling 'Stop! Stop!' 'We can't stop', said one in authority. 'You must stop', responded Mr Lutwidge, with a voice that would have overawed a whole court, and very red with wrath and running . . . Away the monster moved, insolently puffing back his scorn at his pursuers, and soon gave the barristers steam bail.

The luggage was later delivered to Sowerby Bridge on the return train to Leeds, much to the relief of the three advocates. Having passed through the 640 yards long Sowerby Bridge Tunnel, the train entered the sinuous valley of the Calder. *The Railway Times* continued:

> The scenery here, as we passed Luddenden Foot, Mytholmroyd, etc, becomes increasingly beautiful and grand. The railway runs up the west side of the valley, alternately on embankments and through cuttings – the river having in several places been diverted, to save the expense of crossing it by bridges. At 49 minutes past ten o'clock, that is, two hours and 56 minutes after leaving Leeds, we arrived in perfect

safety at Hebden Bridge – a distance of 37 miles [sic] from Leeds, and 23 from Manchester.

Various directors of the Company, with George Stephenson, Thomas Gooch, and Captain John Laws RN (Superintendent of the Line), met the train as it entered Hebden Bridge Station. At 11.45 a.m. they took the return train to Leeds, and apparently unable to contain their desire to travel over the new line, returned in the same afternoon: 'The 11.45 train was crowded to excess, and several of the waggons intended for cattle were filled with third-class passengers'. At Leeds, the Directors ate 'a hasty lunch', and left again for Manchester by the train at 3 o'clock. In the afternoon, a second train ran between Leeds and Hebden Bridge. At Brighouse, an amusing incident occurred which is worth relating in part:

> The second-class carriages were crammed to suffocation, so that extremely few of those who were in could sit . . . A vigorous and determined effort on the part of the railway authorities abated the nuisance, but those who were chased out of the carriages scaled the deck, and soon all were covered . . . Some shrewd person (we suspect Captain Laws) perceiving that this load was too much . . . ordered out a waggon used for the conveyance of cattle, in which those who were on the tops of the carriages were told that they might be accommodated. Instantly, the crews descended the decks and rushed into the cattle waggon, which was crowded to excess; and as soon as this had been accomplished . . . the train cast off the waggon, and moved on at full speed, leaving behind the choused and dismayed cattle, amidst the infinite amusement and applause of the spectators.

So much for the enthusiasm of the public and the *ruse de guerre* of Captain Laws. (Captain Laws of Royal Navy background obviously inspired the writer of the above which alludes to naval terms).

The *Manchester Guardian*, 7 October, already carried a Company notice which had been issued on 29 September:

'The public are respectfully informed, that on and after Monday 5th October 1840, this Line will be FURTHER OPENED for the Conveyance of Passengers, and General Merchandise, between Leeds and Hebden Bridge'. The accompanying table showed that three trains left Hebden Bridge at 8 a.m, 11.30 a.m. and 3.13 p.m., arriving at Leeds at 9.50 a.m., 1.20 p.m. and 5.06 p.m. respectively. In the other direction, three trains left Leeds at 7.45 a.m, 10 a.m and 3 p.m, arriving at Hebden Bridge at 9.36 a.m., 11.50 a.m. and 4.50 p.m. respectively. No trains were operated on Sundays. During the normal operations which followed, only one minor mishap seems to have caused any alarm. *The Railway Times* thought it important enough to make a mention of it in its 24 October edition:

> Wednesday, on the arrival of the last train from Hebden Bridge at the Sowerby Bridge station, for some cause yet unexplained, several of the carriages were thrown off the rails; had it not been that the engine was in the act of stopping at the moment, and close to the walls upon which the shed was to be erected, in all probability the consequences would have been awful.

With both western and eastern sections of the main line open, comprising a total of forty miles of route, there were great expectations of the opening of the remaining nine miles, which included the Summit Tunnel. *The Railway Times*, 17 October, in its conclusion to the long description of the public opening referred to above, declared, 'It is confidently anticipated that this distance of nine miles, the final link in the chain, will be ready for opening in the first week in December, when the trains will pass uninterruptedly from Leeds to Manchester'. This was, of course, stated before the disturbed invert in the Summit Tunnel thwarted the best intentions.

Board of Trade inspection of the unopened part of the line was carried out by Lieut-Colonel Sir Frederic Smith, RE in December 1840. Smith presented his findings to the Lords of the Committee of Privy Council on 23 December, and for the sake of clarity, divided the unopened line into three portions: Littleborough to Summit Tunnel – 1½ miles; the tunnel itself; and the 6 miles 7 furlongs of line between the tunnel and Hebden Bridge station. Both Robert Gill and Thomas Gooch informed Smith that for the present time, 'it is only intended to work over the first section of a mile and a half with goods'. It is supposed that 'with goods' meant that it was intended that materials for completing the tunnel, permanent way, etc, would be conveyed over the short length of the railway. To this, Smith had no objection, 'provided', he said, 'the permanent way be ballasted up, and obvious irregularities in some few parts of the rails be adjusted'. The inspector was cognisant of the failure of the invert at the eastern end of the tunnel, and here he was 'of the opinion that this part of the work will not be completed for upwards of two months; and should then be again inspected'. Passenger traffic was to be worked immediately over the third portion and it was to the latter that Smith concentrated his attention:

> With some important exceptions, I found the cuttings in excellent order, the slopes having been well-formed, and the superfluous earth removed. Mr Gooch undertook forthwith to remedy the defects which I pointed out to him in this respect, as well as to supply ballast where it appeared to me to be deficient.

The defects that Smith alluded to concerned incomplete fencing, distance posts, and the lack of gates at level crossings – the gates being made but not hung. He also referred to the Charlestown Tunnel débâcle, and the need for tight curves to overcome the problem as being the only departure from the Parliamentary approved plan. Smith was impressed by an intimation from Gooch that since the opening of the eastern section between Normanton and Hebden Bridge, and between Manchester and Littleborough, 'not one axle has broken belonging to the Leeds and Manchester Railway. This, in my opinion, is attributable not only to careful driving but also to the iron being of the first quality, namely, from the Low Moor Works'. Smith's inspection was far-reaching. He noticed that the second and third-class carriages in use did not possess spring buffers, and that there were no police on the line. The need for spring buffers was impressed on the Directors as essential safeguards, while the apparent absence of policemen was met with the rejoinder,

> the whole of the platelayers and porters of the Company are constables, and that the consequent vigilance resulting from a pride these men take in thus being placed in authority has been found to supersede the necessity of any more expensive system of surveillance.

Smith regarded this as quite sufficient where traffic was light but not 'where trains are very frequent'.

The report was concluded with a reference to the benefits of the railway to the travelling public.

> I have noticed on this and on former occasions, the desire evinced by the Leeds and Manchester Company to afford the lower classes of the district through which their railway passes the convenience of this mode of travelling, and it appears that they appreciate and avail themselves of it, as the number of third class passengers on this line is to the number of second class as 26 to 6, and the comparison between the number of third class and first class is 26 to 1. The plan adopted is to run with every train carriage of each class; a practice which appears to me to be very commendable. It is also, I find, in contemplation to run goods waggons with every train; when this is done the greatest care must be used in the manufacture of the waggons.

The tunnel was inspected for the second time and pronounced fit for public use throughout on 1 March 1841. *The Railway Times*, five days later, made up for the lack of a formal opening by announcing to all its readers that:

> This line was opened throughout on Monday last. The Directors and a party of their friends, including Mr G. Stephenson, and Mr Gooch as the engineers, made a trip in a special train; starting from the

Manchester station at half-past nine in the morning and proceeding to Normanton where the line joins the North Midland. They were joined at the Summit Tunnel and at Ossett by bands of music. The average speed maintained throughout, exclusive of stoppages, was 30 miles an hour . . . The regular passenger and goods trains commenced running at an early hour and several passed through the tunnel before the half-past nine o'clock special train.

Herapath's Journal, 13 March, somewhat behind in its report on the opening, nevertheless found space in its columns to describe details of the special train.

> The train consisted of two carriages; both being of an entirely new construction, but somewhat different from each other. The body of one of them is 18 feet by 7, and is 6 feet 6 ins high. There is a compartment in the centre seven feet square, and is built in the fashion of a gondola. The interior of this compartment is fitted up with splendid mahogany sofas, lined with crimson plush, and trimmed with silk gymp; and the

top part above the sofa boxes is comprised of plate glass with silk curtains. The two end compartments are open above; but a curtain made of waterproof fabric can be drawn down at pleasure to screen the passengers from the rain, so that in these carriages a person may enjoy all the comforts of a first-class carriage; and at the same time, be enabled to survey the country through which he is passing. The other carriage, the Tourist, is similar in its general arrangements, but is fitted up differently. These carriages, which were made by Mr Mellings, of Greenheys, are adapted for summer travelling; there are but two of them, and they are merely for an experiment.

Soon after the opening of the complete railway, a serious accident occurred to blot the Company's excellent record. On Friday 26 March, the 4 p.m. passenger train toiled out of the Manchester station. It was a particularly heavy train, for attached to the rear were four loaded wagons. To assist the train up the stiff gradients as far as Mills Hill, a second locomotive, the *Humber*, was used as a banker. Having reached a point one mile beyond Mills Hill, the banker dropped back, stopped and then returned on the same line back to Manchester – the driver hoping to stable his engine at the shed before the passage of a second train which had left. The *Manchester Guardian*, on the 31 March, pointedly remarked that:

> This . . . was a direct violation of the regulations, a printed copy of which is furnished to every person employed on the line. The regulation in question is as follows – Every locomotive engine shall pass along the proper line of road, which is invariably to be the left-hand of the permanent way, either going from or returning towards Manchester. Any engineman disobeying this order will be immediately discharged, and will be subject to punishment under Lord Seymour's Act.

The returning banker, travelling wrong line, arrived at Moston, and was met by the luggage train proceeding up-gradient from

Manchester. Despite braking and reversing the wheels, the fast-approaching luggage train collided with the banker 'which completely smashed the tender of the *Humber* to pieces'. The banker driver was thrown from the footplate and died shortly afterwards on arrival by lorry at his home. The luggage-train driver, and the firemen of both engines, had lain on the coke in the tenders and escaped injury. The *Guardian's* report concluded with, 'The luggage train was stopped for upwards of two hours by the engine being disabled . . . We understand the damage done to the two engines amounts to about £250'. No blame was attributed to the Company – the deceased driver of the banking engine alone posthumously bearing all responsibility for not returning by the correct line in accordance with the Company rules.

The opening of the main line had not been celebrated in any formal way. It was as though, having completed the last nine miles which had delayed a possible earlier opening, the Company attached far more importance to commencing the service promptly and thereby making the railway a fully revenue-earning enterprise. Even so, as the 1841 winter turned into spring, the great achievement was at last recognised. *The Railway Times*, on 3 April, made reference to a minor celebratory function:

> On Monday last, the engineers of the Manchester and Leeds Railway invited Mr Gooch, the heads of their department, to dine with them at the Albion Hotel, Manchester, for the purpose of presenting to him an elegant service of plate as a testimonial to his professional abilities, and a grateful acknowledgment of the kindness and courtesy of his conduct. Some excellent and appropriate speeches were made on the occasion, illustrative of the difficulties unprecedented in the annals of engineering which have been encountered in the construction of this railway, and congratulations to Mr Gooch on his successful accomplishment of the same.

Meanwhile, at the Manchester terminus, efforts were being made to put the finishing touches to the freight capacity at the Oldham Road Station. *The Railway Times*, 3 April 1841, following events there, described the outcome of the activities:

> No fewer than 12 of the arches are now occupied by various carriers and completely fitted up with every convenience to enable them to transmit goods on the line. The Directors have spared no expense and to avoid the never-ending labour that must have occurred in hoisting up by hand-cranes the immense quantities of goods that are now despatched. A steam engine has been erected for that purpose, but instead of raising each single bale or cask, a waggon is loaded beneath with its full complement of goods, back-sheeted, etc, ready to start for its destination.

Passengers going to and from the station (which was on a higher level than the goods yard) found that in addition to the usual hustle and bustle, the incessant confusion of goods in transit, being lifted, lowered, turned, sheeted up, moved forwards and backwards, caused no small measure of annoyance, and to some extent danger. From this, the public were now saved as they approached or left the station area.

Later the same month, an incident occurred at Oldham Road Station, involving an apprentice at the station's engine shed. The young man had climbed aboard a simmering locomotive after its arrival from Leeds with a luggage train. The careless engineman had left the locomotive in an improper condition, with the brakes off, but the steam not off. *The Railway Times*, 24 April, dealt with the story thus:

> Probably, not understanding the engine, the boy set it in motion and it darted forward, broke through the wall of the shed, and fell a height of about 20 feet into the field below where it was deeply embedded in clay. It lay there until about six o'clock next morning when it was got out and it appeared that the damage done to it was very trifling . . . The boy got off the engine, no one knows how, and has not been seen since.

One of the consequences of the controversial Lord Seymour's Act of October 1840 was that each railway company was obliged to submit a detailed return to the Board of Trade, under the Act 3 and 4 Vic. c.97 s.3. The essence of this specific of the Act read, 'Returns . . . of the aggregate traffic in passengers, according to the several classes, and of the aggregate traffic in cattle and goods respectively'. Such a return was made to the Board of Trade by the M&L and was made known publicly by *The Railway Times*, 19 June 1841, and thus provides us with a picture of the working railway in its early days:

> All mixed trains; 10 trains per day each way, except Sunday, when there are four trains each way. Number of passengers – First Class, 16,124; Second Class, 72,325; Third Class, 311,335. Total mileage of each class – First, 265,969; Second, 850,747; Third, 2,349,269. Average fare per mile – First Class, 3d; Second Class, 2d; Third Class, 1d; Gross receipts from passengers – First Class, £3,609 4s 3d; Second Class, £8,119 6s 11d; Third Class, £13,163 0s 3d; total, £24,891 11s 5d. Goods, horses, etc, carried at the same rate as passengers. Rates per mile: horses, 3d each; carriages, 6d; cattle, 2d; sheep, 1d to 5d; pigs, 7d to 16d.

Towards the end of 1841, John Herapath had the opportunity to travel over the line between Leeds and Manchester, accompanied by Captain Laws, the General Manager, and Robert Gill, Managing Director, the three of them riding in the opulent 'Gondola' carriage. His observations are an appropriate way of concluding this chapter on the openings and workings of the railway. Apart from the spectacular scenery through which the train passed, Herapath was also impressed by the populous areas:

> It is as if it was one continued town. I am informed that taking in three miles each side of the line, the population amounts to 1,000,000. Hence there is a great local traffic, of which nothing can deprive the railway . . . Every effort which can be made by the manager in chief, Captain Laws, is made to nurse and mature this traffic . . . In goods their traffic is very great.

Herapath was also impressed by the business-like appearance of the offices; of these, it was obvious that the Company had spent money wisely on the bare essentials, and not on unnecessary ornamentation. The principle of thrift had, perhaps, carried too far, for he commented that, 'Even the principal station at Manchester is destitute of ornament'. The Summit Tunnel also drew opinion from him:

> I had the opportunity of riding through it one way on the engine, and was much pleased with the smoothness of the brickwork, and the dryness of the tunnel. In going through . . . two torches are generally lighted on the engine and tender, which, though they are no substitute for daylight, afford some comfort to the passengers.

On 2 January 1841, his own publication *Railway Magazine and Commercial Journal* had mentioned the intention of the Company to install a means of communication in the tunnel, 'a telegraph from one end to the other, which will probably be a pneumatic telegraph; by which means, intelligence may be communicated from one mouth to the other, of the approach, entrance, and exit of trains'.

The very last word should be reserved for Thomas Gooch who remained the Company's engineer until June 1844 when he was superseded by John Hawkshaw. A report which reached *Herapath's Journal* in time for the 25 September 1841 edition, was one of his last in connection with the M&L Railway. This read:

> The main line having been opened throughout on 1st March last, I have the satisfaction of being able to report that the trains have continued to run without interruption or accident, that the whole of the works on the line remain in a very satisfactory state, all in good order and condition, and I see the prospect of my former statements as to the cheap cost of maintenance being realised.

Perhaps he had forgotten, or chose to forget, the accident of 26 March 1841, mentioned earlier.

SIX

Trouble with the Sabbath

The most important influence on the Victorian Sunday was English Sabbatarianism. It appeared to consist of a perverse reluctance to enjoy oneself on Sundays and a determination to stop other people enjoying themselves too.[43]

EVERY age has its over-zealous preoccupation with denigrating anything new and different, anything, that is, perceived by some to be a threat to the foundations of everyday life. This appears to have been so in the late 1830s and 1840s when, as the incipient railway system was finding its feet, the opponents of Sunday travel by train were at their most vociferous. Opposition was such that the railway protagonists were abashed by the weight of the Sabbatarian argument, and this can be felt in the following observation made by *The Railway Times*:

> The uncharitable spirit in which railways have been treated by so many well-meaning and really worthy persons is additional proof of the tendency of human nature to quarrel with all that is new, and to assume that because a thing is at variance with our established habits, it must of necessity be bad.[44]

The Lord's Day Observance Society was formed on 8 February 1831 under the auspices of Daniel and Joseph Wilson. It quickly gathered adherents in the form of well-educated individuals whose background ranged from religious clergy to at least one Member of Parliament. Drawing upon the Fourth Commandment of the Decalogue, the Sabbatarians formalised their pursuit in a central committee with auxiliaries, or local bodies actively pursuing the same cause throughout England. The upper classes largely kept out of the movement, whilst the lower classes, were generally excluded from the Society by reason of their inability or unwillingness to pay the annual subscription. According to John Wigley, 'The Lord's Day Observance Society, with an annual subscription of 10s 6d, was mainly middle class, with a small number of bishops and MPs and a handful of gentry and aristocracy'.[45]

The disciple of Sunday Observance followed a set of principles which were expected of him; Roger Homer expressed these succinctly as follows:

> he should attend church or chapel at least once on Sunday; he will wear his Sunday best; he must abstain from secular entertainments; he must spend the day in religious conversation and though and in the performance of certain good works; he must confine his reading to suitable literature, much of which was produced for the purpose. [46]

The thought of travelling by train on Sunday (as distinct from travelling by road or upon water) was held an anathema, a direct contravention of the Fourth Commandment.

Sabbatarians drew their convictions from biblical theology which they expounded with energy; denunciation of those railways on which Sunday trains operated incurred the epithet 'Devil's Highway'. Such leading lights as Sir Andrew Agnew, MP (this gentleman alone attracting many disciples – the 'Agnewites'), and the Reverend Francis Close, vicar of

43. John Wigley, *The Rise and Fall of the Sunday*, p.2.

44. *The Railway Times*, 4 April 1840.

45. John Wigley, ibid, p.43.

46. Roger Homer, *Sunday Observance and Social Class*, p.81.

Cheltenham, plus an number of Scottish Presbyterian clergy, were successful in making life difficult for the newly-established railway companies. Often, in order to placate those shareholders who had Sabbatarian sympathies, and as a sop to local objectors, some railway companies ran their Sunday trains outside church-going hours, in what became known as the 'Church Interval'.

There were, however, counter arguments in support of Sunday trains and travel. Mail trains, whether carrying passengers or not, were expected to operate on Sundays: an Act of Parliament had been passed on 14 August 1838 – 'An Act to provide for the Conveyance of the Mail by Railways' – and obliged the companies to carry mail on a 28-days notice principle, inclusive of Sundays. (Agnew had persuaded the Post Office not to run the stage coaches which carried the mail in his constituency of Wigtownshire but this was a unique situation). As far as the popular railway excursions were concerned, they were regarded by social reformers as a means of enabling the mass of working people to escape their six days of labour and find solace in brighter, fresher and more healthy surroundings – a benefit recognised by enlightened reformers but which the Sabbatarians sought to deny. As one writer on the subject has observed:

> During the 1840s company after company had replied to Sabbatarian enthusiasts who interrupted their shareholders meetings that Sunday trains enabled the working classes to visit the countryside and to refresh themselves innocently and soberly. Much of the railway interest regarded itself as the agent of social progress which the Sabbatarians were trying to obstruct.[47]

The Railway Times, between 1838 and 1847, printed both sides of the argument. Several letters appeared in the July and August 1841 editions from 'An Anti-Sunday Transitarian', each epistle replete with a long-winded theological discussion purporting to give reasons why Sunday train travel was sinful. At first the journal was tolerant of these opinions, but nevertheless failed to understand why railway journeys were singled out as being contrary to the Will of God. 'It would

seem, indeed, as if there was something peculiarly desecrating in the passage of a locomotive train along a district previously traversed by a dozen or more stage coaches.'[48] Increasingly after 1842, the same journal became more irritated by what it termed 'bigoted cant'. Such irritation can be felt in the following extracts taken from the April 1843 edition:

> We understand that a memorial has been addressed to certain inhabitants of Colchester to the Directors of the Eastern Counties Railway complaining of the number of trains appointed to run on Sundays. We trust that the Directors will not be influenced by these disciples of that obsolete gentleman, Sir A. Agnew, but will attend as much on Sunday, as on Monday, or Saturday, to the convenience of the public.[49]

One year later the Agnewites were busy in Scotland trying to impose their doctrine on the Edinburgh & Glasgow Railway, which had been opened on 21 February 1842. By 1844, *The Railway Times* had had enough of Sir Andrew Agnew as the following extract illustrates: 'Is there no end to this rant and cant against the Edinburgh & Glasgow Railway? The concern is flourishing in spite of all the denunciations of the Agnewites against it'. Despite all their efforts, the Agnewites, even with their mentor in the van, 'have no more chance of stopping it than they have of getting back to the manses they have deserted in a free fit of ecclesiastical delusion'.[50]

How did the Sabbatarian attitude towards the railways affect the M&L? It will be recalled that the Company had already been accused of 'Profanation of the Sabbath' (CHAPTER 3) in September 1838, and on that occasion had refuted such claims in a speedy response. Employing labour on a Sunday was one thing; the running of trains was quite another. With the partial opening of the line between Manchester and Littleborough, no Sunday service was available. The question of Sunday trains was raised, however, at a general half-yearly meeting of shareholders on 12 September 1839, and according to *Herapath*, this was an important occasion:

> There was a very numerous attendance, every seat in

47. John Wigley, ibid, p.85.

48. *The Railway Times*, 13 March 1841.

49. Ibid, 8 April 1843.

50. Ibid, 20 April 1844.

the room being filled, and a number of gentlemen being compelled to remain standing. In addition to regular business . . . notice had been given in the circular convening the meeting, that the subject of opening the portion of the line already completed, from Manchester to Littleborough, on Sundays, would be taken into consideration . . . The general interest excited by this question, caused the attendance to be much more numerous . . . a great number of shareholders from a distance having come over for the purpose.[51]

To the assembled shareholders, the Chairman, James Wood, read out the circular and threw open the question of Sunday trains for discussion. Those who could not attend the meeting in person 'were requested to send their proxies' five days before the meeting took place. Three propositions were put forward for consideration, namely: 'First, the railway should be closed on Sunday; second, that it should be partially opened for passengers; and third, that it should be opened for passengers without restriction'.[52] The proxy votes alone, which had been counted before the meeting, showed an outcome decidedly in favour of the second proposition, but it was felt that much discussion was needed at the meeting so that opinions could be expressed prior to a final show of hands. Extended discussion occurred involving such M&L notables as James Wood, Henry Houldsworth, Robert Gill, James Heald, and the Todmorden textile magnate (and director) John Fielden. It was the latter who, as an employer of many in his cotton mills, had firm ideas as to whether trains should run on Sundays, remarking to loud applause that 'The Sabbath was made for man, not man for the Sabbath'.

> The best plan, as it appeared to him, would be to allow the line to be open in the morning and the evening; and it would be the passengers themselves who would be the desecrators of the Sabbath, if any desecration took place. He strongly objected to the Company compelling anyone to work on the Sabbath. He should give his support to the second proposition. [53]

John Fielden's speech hinted at the adoption of the 'Church Interval', which was a convenient expedient for the Company, whilst in order to avoid the accusation of Sabbath-breaking, the onus would be on the travelling public instead of the Company. In the event, the second proposition was adopted by the gathering, a show of hands indicating a majority of three to one. It must have been something of a bombshell when, as a result of this decision three of the directors resigned. *The Railway Times*, 23 September 1839, regretted their decision and went on to explain why James Wood, James Heald and John Barker had taken such a drastic step: 'These gentlemen, we understand, assented to the principle of a morning and evening train for purposes of necessity but the attempt to accommodate their views to those of brother directors was unsuccessful and their resignation was the consequence'.

The following accounts reveal that public demand for a Sunday service was real enough. The *Manchester Chronicle*, 21 September 1839, had this to report:

> In consequence of the opening of the railway for Sunday travelling the village of Littleborough experienced on Sunday last a considerable accession of company. They were mostly clerks, warehousemen, and the decenter sort of operatives, with some females and children, the two latter fewer in number probably in consequence of the broken weather. The day passed off without the least irregularity or disturbance, and not a small proportion of the visitors attended services in the afternoon at the church.

Again, the *Manchester Guardian*, 5 October, the same year:

> Great numbers continue to avail themselves of the opening of the Manchester and Leeds Railroad for the purpose of enjoying the pure air in the mountainous neighbourhood of Rochdale. All the inns as well as the eating houses at Littleborough were again crowded on Sunday. Numbers ascended the ridge of the great vertebrae of England, Blackstone Edge, from

51. *Herapath*, 14 September 1839.
52. Ibid.
53. Ibid.

whence they could obtain a very extended view over Lancashire, as well, probably, as a good appetite for whatever refreshment might fall in their way.

The first public timetable attendant upon the opening of the line between Manchester and Littleborough stated that there were no trains running on Sundays. As soon as the decision had been made to run them, the new timetable, as from 15 September, indicated that there were four trains in both directions, two in the morning and two in the evening, all scheduled so as not to infringe the Church Interval, taking that to lie between 10 a.m. and 1 p.m. When the line between Leeds and Hebden Bridge opened, timetables as from 5 and 26 October 1840 followed the same pattern as the opening between Manchester and Littleborough, that is, 'no trains on Sundays for the present'. It was not until the full opening of the line that the services as from 1 March 1841 included four Sunday trains in both directions, two of which were mail trains. By this time, the Company had apparently decided to waive the restrictions of the Church Interval, two of its trains departing and completing their journeys within that time. No doubt the Company believed in John Fielden's notion that the passengers and not the Company were responsible for breaking the Sabbath. Some adjustment to the March services occurred the following month. Issued on 12 April, the timetable showed that Sunday traffic had been reduced to three trains in both directions (again two being mail trains) although such a modification was probably a response to the public's

travelling preferences. Reference to Bradshaw's railway timetables, 1842–47, reveal that very few changes in the number of Sunday trains running in both directions were made, although the actual departure times varied within any one year, and in different years. TABLE A shows the frequency of trains over a five-year period, the fastest service between Manchester and Leeds, and vice versa, being the mails, completing their journeys in 2 hours 50 minutes – cheaper, slower trains, stopping at every station, taking between 3 and 3½ hours.

Throughout the period 1840–47, arguments for and against Sunday train services prevailed and yet, seemingly undeterred, the MLR, along with other companies, decided to run them anyway. The companies were emboldened by the demand by the public and the Parliamentary call for such services to continue. According to Jack Simmons, 'Out of this welter of disputation a general policy emerged in England and Wales of providing some Sunday trains on most main lines, as well as on a number of branches'.[54] The pattern of Sunday traffic was already established by 1840, regardless of the censorious disapproval of the Sabbatarians. Certainly by the mid-1840s, the M&L felt free to run as many trains as perceived to be necessary to fulfil public needs. Although Sabbatarianism was far from moribund in the late 1840s, its past failure to receive Parliamentary support permitted the railway companies to provide both scheduled services and excursions; these were to the benefit of the Company (by way of increased profits), the public (by way of increased mobility), and the country as a whole (by social and economic improvement).

54. Jack Simmons, *The Victorian Railway*, p.284.

YEAR	MANCHESTER TO LEEDS DEPARTURE TIMES	LEEDS TO MANCHESTER DEPARTURE TIMES
1842	8 a.m; 10.50 a.m; 6.30 p.m; 10 p.m.	8 a.m; 10.16 a.m; 6 p.m; 7.15 p.m.
1843	8 a.m; 10.50 a.m; 5 p.m; 6.30 p.m.	7 a.m; 10.10 a.m; 7.15 p.m.
1844 June	8 a.m; 10.50 a.m; 7.15 p.m.	7 a.m; 10.10 a.m; 7.15 p.m.
1844 Oct.	8 a.m; 10.50 a.m; 7.30 p.m.	7 a.m; 10.40 a.m; 7.15 p.m.
1845 Feb.	8 a.m; 10.50 a.m; 7.30 p.m.	7 a.m; 10.40 a.m; 7.30 p.m.
1845 June	8 a.m; 10.15 a.m; 7.30 p.m.	7 a.m; 10.40 a.m; 7.30 p.m.
1846 Feb.	8 a.m; 10.15 a.m; 5 p.m; 7.30 p.m.	7 a.m; 10.40 a.m; 6.10 p.m; 8 p.m.
1847 June	ditto	ditto

TABLE A: Frequency of services on the M&L over a five-year period, 1842–47

SEVEN

The Hunt's Bank Extension and Victoria Station

T HE fate of the Oldham Road terminus was sealed in 1838, two years before its completion, when the M&L Company envisaged its railway forming a chain of communication between Liverpool and Hull. They determined to form a connection with the already functioning L&M Railway. On 31 March, George Stephenson, speaking of the unfinished railway at a half-yearly meeting, remarked that:

> By this conveyance, all pilferage will be avoided, and the journey will be completed, from Manchester to Hull, in a few hours, whilst the route by canal occupies many days . . . This railway will also take a portion of the traffic from the Leeds and Liverpool Canal, so as soon as a convenient junction is formed with the Liverpool and Manchester Railway . . . this route will be in favour of the railway for traffic going from Ireland to the Continent.[55]

The projected junction line would involve a central station at Hunt's Bank, land for which had been purchased for, and presented to the Company in August 1838 by Samuel Brooks, the M&L Vice-Chairman and noted city banker.

In a letter addressed to the M&L Board in August 1838, Samuel Brooks made it clear that he was willing to sell land to the Company in order that it could construct the Hunt's Bank connection. The letter read as follows:

> I beg to inform you that I have purchased the plot of land near to Hunt's Bank, for which I had been in treaty for a long time before it was contemplated that your station would be there. The purport of this letter is to say, that if you require any portion of that land, you shall have it on reasonable terms; I pledge myself that the Company shall not be prejudiced by its being in my hands. I have refrained from selling it, till I know whether the Company would want it or not. I had some offers for it already.

This was a gift to the Company, a 'handsome offer' as James Wood described it, and one which his fellow directors had agreed to take advantage of.

Though seemingly a straightforward scheme, it was to be subjected to an inordinate measure of procrastination by the Liverpool company for the next four years. The essence of this company's hesitation to collaborate fully with the M&L lay in its counter-proposal for a looping southern line which would facilitate a connection to be made with the temporary Manchester and Birmingham station at Store Street. Such a scheme also had the support of the highly influential Bridgewater Trustees over whose land it would pass. According to one authority on the subject,

> The fact that the projected Oldham Road to London Road link would have necessitated a 1,160 yard tunnel, the trans-shipment of goods by crane between the stations to be built at London Road, and would be virtually useless to the Manchester & Leeds company, as a through route . . . gave the tunnel project a positive merit in the eyes of the Liverpool & Manchester directors.[56]

55. *The Railway Times*, 24 March 1838.

56. J.R. Kellett, *Railways and Victorian Cities*, p.170.

The northern end of Victoria Station at Hunt's Bank constituted a single-storey building as shown in the Tait lithograph (see p.44). At some time not yet ascertained the single storey was heightened by the addition of a further level, whilst the front of the same assumed a new appearance. Far right is the L&Y station building designed by William Dawes, integrated with that of the M&L, and completed in 1904. Far left is the continuation of the M&L's station frontage which faced on to Hunt's Bank. Photographed July 1997 by the author

The four years of wrangle over which route was the most economical to construct, and the best to serve the needs of the companies and the public, were characterised by disagreement, frustration, and acrimony. Four railway companies were involved, along with the Mersey & Irwell Navigation Company, and the Bridgewater Trustees. Yet throughout these years, the M&L Company never lost sight of its principal aim of constructing an extension line from Miles Platting to Hunt's Bank, and the provision of a new station. An application to Parliament for these had received Royal Assent on 1 July 1839, and at the well-attended half-yearly meeting on 5 September, James Heald, one of the Directors, read the following as part of his report to the assembly:

> The Directors beg to announce their successful application in the past session of Parliament, for powers to form branches to Oldham and Halifax, and also the important junction with the Liverpool and Manchester, and Bolton and Bury Railways, thereby securing to the towns of Manchester and Salford, both to communications and stations, advantages superior to any other towns in the kingdom, shortening the distance fully one-third from Liverpool to Hull . . . and, presenting the convenience of setting down passengers at the junction stations, within 500 yards of the Exchange.

Henry Houldsworth, the M&L Chairman, saw not only the benefits of having a station within a short distance of the Exchange, but also the advantages to be gained from what he called 'omnibus traffic': 'It is of great advantage to us that our line comes within one hundred yards of Shudehill, where all the short coaches and stages stand'.[57] He also observed the nearness of the navigable Irwell, for he continued: 'We have also the advantage of coming down to the river; and the Old Quay Company have lately passed a resolution to survey the river, with a view to bringing the navigation to this point'.[58] The Old Quay Company was a colloquial name for the Mersey & Irwell Navigation Company with which, it was alleged, the holders of 87.5% of the stock had agreed to tranship to barges.

Not until the autumn of 1841 however, amidst a welter of indecision and manoeuvrings of the Liverpool Company did the M&L Company decide to press ahead with its scheme. At the half-yearly meeting held on 16 September, Mr Entwistle, a Director, expressed his opinions about the lack of progress:

> The continued indispostion of the Directors of the Liverpool and Manchester Railway Company to proceed with its connection line together with the unfavourable state of the times, and the serious inconvenience which would be caused to the proprietors by calling on them for any large amount of capital under the great depression . . . has combined to deter the Directors from submitting to the shareholders . . . any proposition for the immediate commencement of the works upon the Extension line to Hunt's Bank.

It was felt, however, that the M&L Company should act quickly before the powers to purchase land expired in the following July.

Finding itself bereft of the support of the Manchester & Birmingham Railway, threatened with a projected railway to Liverpool (sponsored by the M&L, along with other companies), and the prospect of the increased conveyance of goods by the Old Quay Company, the L&M Directors finally assented to the Hunt's Bank scheme. The *Manchester Guardian*, 4 May

57. *Herapath*, 21 March 1840. There were plans to enlarge and improve the Irwell and Mersey navigation and to construct new wharves in order to bring goods directly to the Hunt's Bank Station.

58. Ibid.

1842, carried the following contracts for work, the indication now being that the work was to start without further delay:

Contract No.1. The formation and completion of the junction line from a point about four chains east of Collyhurst Lane to the east side of Lower Tebbutt Street in the town of Manchester, being a distance of about 1,316 yards; including the formation of the excavations and embankments, the building of arches over the reservoirs near Collyhurst; the bridge over Collyhurst Lane; bridges with iron girders under St. George's Road and Cropper Street; retaining walls drains, laying and ballasting the permanent way under the works connected therewith.

Contract No.2. The formation and completion of the said junction line from the termination of the last contract to the intended station at Hunt's Bank, being a distance of about 706 yards. This contract consists principally of a viaduct containing several bridges with iron girders, and crosses some of the principal streets in Manchester as well as passing three times over the River Irk.

Engineer's Office 22nd April 1842

Both contracts were awarded to John Brogden on 6 June, and work began two weeks later. On 15 June, the *Manchester Guardian* was able to report that the railway company had 'broken ground in York Street, Cheetham, in preparation for excavating the ground for the line'. The construction of the viaducts and bridges was of such magnitude that the area through which the Extension was to pass had to be cleared of existing properties: 'A number of cottage tenants . . . have received notices to quit; many of the weekly tenants have already left and the cottages have been pulled down . . . All is bustle in the neighbourhood and the preparations for commencing the works are being made with all expedition'. According to Friedrich Engels, the railway extension passed through one of the worst slum areas of Manchester, an area known as New Town, which lay between the river Irk and St

George's Road. The area of wretched hovels of the worst kind was relieved by equally dismal and squalid passages and adjoining yards: 'The newly built extension of the Leeds Railway, which crosses the Irk here, has swept away some of these courts and lanes, laying others completely open to view'.[59] It would seem from Engel's description of New Town that the appearance of the Extension line, far from disrupting and despoiling the area through which it passed, actually promoted destruction of parts of the veritable shanty town which had long lay adjacent to the old Manchester town centre.

The rapid construction was not without incident. Late October and early November 1842 were very wet, the copious rain having deleterious effects on the setting of the mortar binding the bridges and arches. The *Manchester Courier*, 29 October, reported 'an accident of a very alarming nature', alluding to the arches of the Extension-line viaduct: 'The greatest consternation was excited in the neighbourhood on Thursday afternoon by the sudden fall of one of these arches . . . This arch has been completed and the centres taken out about a week before; and it was considered a very perfect piece of work'. What had caused a perfectly sound arch to collapse? The construction referred to by the *Manchester Courier* drew the attention of Thomas Gooch, no less, who was questioned by the Chairman about the unfortunate incident. The involvement of Gooch quickly elicited the reasons. The timber centres which supported the arch had been authorised to be slacked but not removed. Perhaps in haste, the contractor's men removed the centres and 'neglected to load both ends of the arch equally'. This, coupled with the heavy rains which had saturated the mortar, had caused some strain on one side of the arch, which brought the whole structure crashing down. Men had been working above the arch when it fell a height of 14 feet, but apart from bruising and one broken thigh, there was no more serious harm done. Thus the blame lay on John Brogden, the contractor, who was so heavily involved in the Extension scheme.

At the head of the Extension line, a stationary engine house was to be erected under the direction of a Mr Walker, (James Walker?), his tender of £2,870 being accepted by the

59. Friedrich Engels, *Condition of the Working Class in England*, p.4.

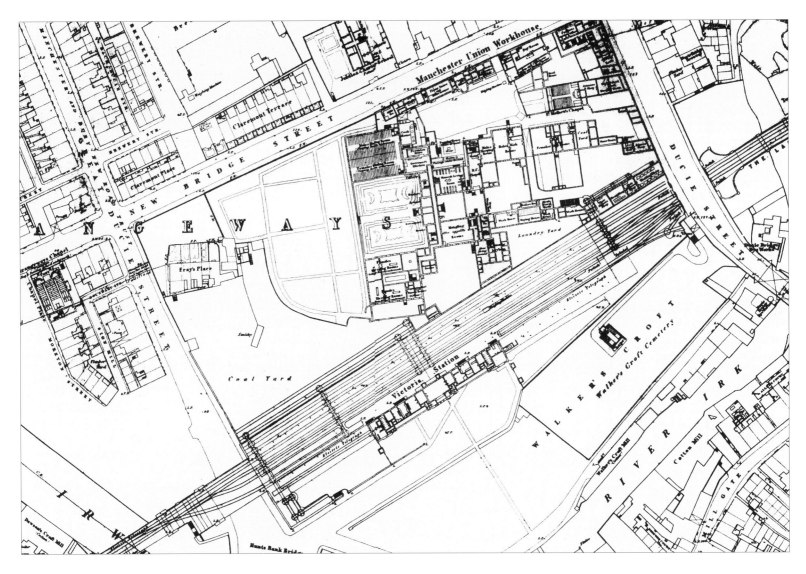

The layout of Victoria Station, Manchester, surveyed by Captain Tucker and published in 1848

Company on 23 January 1843. A 240 h.p. double engine was to work the endless cable which would haul the trains up the steep incline out of the Hunt's Bank station. Even here, there were eventual problems with the engine-house construction. On 25 April 1843, it was reported that the contractor was not proceeding satisfactorily and that some danger to the main line was anticipated due to the unskilful manner in which

he was excavating so close to the main line. Once again, Gooch had to take measures to remedy the situation.

Closely associated with the Extension was the building of the new joint station at Hunt's Bank; John Brogden, despite his unauthorised removal of the centres of the arch, won the contract at a price of £19,000, this being accepted on 6 March 1843. The site chosen for the station involved major changes to the layout of the areas around the station, and in October 1842, preparations were being made for the eventual erection of the building. The *Manchester Guardian*, reported fully on these in its 12 October edition:

> We see that a row of houses in Hunt's Bank are already taken down, and we understand that it is intended to raise the level of the road over Hunt's Bank bridge four feet to have an inclined approach to the line which will be considerably above the level of the road ... the railway being over Ducie Street by an iron bridge from a point just beyond the Castle Inn. The river Irk is to be arched over for an extent of 30 yards to give facility to this approach which will wind round by Walker's Croft.

The old mansion at Hunt's Bank, which had served as the Company's headquarters, was due for demolition, and arrangements were made to transfer to temporary offices at the Oldham Road Station. The *Manchester Guardian* described the Liverpool Company's approach to the scheme and concluded by adding:

> This slow progression forms a striking contrast to the way in which the works on the other side of the river are advancing; and we understand it is expected that the Leeds Extension line will have the rails laid down to the point where the Hunt's Bank Station commences in the present year.[60]

Within a period of eighteen months, the Extension line and the station at Hunt's Bank had been completed. Major General Pasley inspected the newly-completed works on 29 December 1843. Accompanied by Henry Houldsworth, Chairman, Robert Gill, Managing Director, William Entwistle, Deputy Chairman, and Gooch, Pasley was conveyed by special train, which left the station at 10 o'clock, to the top of the Extension line. From this point, he returned on foot to the station, not along the rails, but by the streets below, inspecting the underside of the viaducts and bridges. On arriving at the station, he travelled by light engine along

the Extension in order to inspect the stationary engine house. 'General Pasley expressed himself very well satisfied with the solid and substantial character of the works generally and gave the usual sanction to the Company to open the line at any time'.[61]

The total length of the Extension was 1 mile 560 yards, the ruling gradients descending to Hunt's Bank station being 1 in 47, and 1 in 59. The line 'dipped' under York Street bridge and then gently ascended to the station along a gradient of 1 in 132. It was envisaged that trains would approach the single platform under their own momentum, and without the need for harsh braking, be brought to a standstill alongside the arrival platform, their speed having been checked by the uphill gradient and by the judicious use of brake vans. Strong buffer stops were nevertheless fixed at the end of the arrival line in case of over-run. Departing trains descended the 1 in 132 gradient and, pausing under York Street bridge, were attached to the endless stranded iron cable, and hauled up the incline by the stationary engine at Miles Platting. This procedure lasted but eighteen months, becoming unnecessary owing to the increased power of locomotives.[62]

A novel feature of the Extension line was the employment of Cooke and Wheatstone's patent electric telegraph. *The*

Before the opening of Victoria Station, Oldham Road Station served as the Company's premier station from the opening of the first section of line in July 1839. Passengers had to negotiate a flight of stairs to reach the booking hall which was 28ft above the surrounding yard. The railway between Miles Platting and the station was carried on a viaduct of 58 arches over a distance of half a mile. Two of the final arches can be seen to the right of the main building, although these were sealed up by the L&Y. Photographed in 1908. Author's Collection

60. *Manchester Guardian*, 12 October 1842

61. Ibid, 3 January 1844.

62. John Marshall, *Lancashire & Yorkshire Railway*, Vol.1, p.57.

Railway Times, 20 January 1844, explained how the telegraph would be used:

> The uses of the telegraph . . . will be threefold:
>
> 1st, To give the signal, from York Street, when the train is attached to the endless rope, to the fixed engine to commence drawing the train up the incline, and also to communicate from the junction to York Street bridge, when a train is arriving.
>
> 2nd, To communicate from the Victoria station to the locomotive engine house, so as to specify whether any or what engines are wanted, etc.
>
> 3rd, Generally to communicate intelligence and directions between the Victoria station and the junction with the main line.

The 'junction' here refers to the point where the original line down to Oldham Road Station joined the Extension line. The telegraph system was to be installed along the entire line, work commencing on the project at the beginning of 1847. The *Manchester Guardian*, 17 February of that year, recognised the fact as follows: 'We are glad to learn that the workmen in the employ of the Electric Telegraph Company are busily engaged in laying the wires along the whole extent of this line from the Victoria station, Hunt's Bank, to Normanton'.

The opening of the Victoria Station on New Year's Day 1844 created a minor sensation in Manchester. The *Manchester Guardian,* on 3 January, gave full vent to an appraisal of what would have been a masterpiece of public amenity engineering.

> This handsome building in what is termed the Roman Doric style, is only one storey in height above the ground and is about 266 feet long by 36 feet in width. The material used in its erection is a description of a wall stone, much used in the West Riding of Yorkshire, though we believe this is the first instance of its use for building in this town or neighbourhood. It is procured at Brighouse, and is usually called 'parr-

point' (pierre-point); it is, in fact, a flagstone broken into small blocks which are of uniform and good colour.

It is fitting to note that a good Yorkshire stone was used in the construction of the company's principal station, in the heart of Lancashire's premier city. The *Guardian* continued:

> The westerly half of this building and indeed of the whole station will be occupied by the Liverpool and Manchester Railway Company; the other half to the east, is now in use by the Manchester and Leeds Railway Company. Approaching the south front of the station by the inclined plane, the visitor finds himself opposite its centre, which projects a little from the line of the building and which is the refreshment saloon for the first and second-class passengers, with ladies waiting rooms, etc. The centre presents a frontage of about 60 feet; the refreshment room is lighted by handsome circular windows, with stone pilasters and dressings, and surmounted by an elegant cornice, about the centre of which is to be placed a large clock. To the right and left respectively are the booking offices of the two companies having entrances under a covered way, supported by brackets nine feet six inches long . . . At the east and west ends of the building are the offices and the residences of the station masters, which project to the same face as the central portion of the building, with handsome doorways and cornices to correspond.

As to the train shed itself:

> The platforms are very large and convenient. That in front of the building is 24 feet wide (of which each company occupies one half), and this is continued towards Liverpool, past the west end of the building, to the length of 184 feet, by 12 feet wide; being, in fact, a continuation of the Liverpool departure platform. Towards Leeds, the platform is continued for 120 feet, by 12 feet wide; being also a continuation of the Leeds departure platform.

The length of each departure platform is about 320 feet . . . At each end of the station . . . is a place where horses and carriages, for conveyance by railway, going to or arriving from the east or west, may be embarked or landed on the level, with every facility.

To protect all from the vagaries of the Manchester weather an overall roof extended across the platforms, encompassing an area of some 80,000 square feet.

Public safety and comfort at was a major consideration. At a Committee of Management meeting on 4 January 1844 it was decreed that the new station should possess an additional gas lamp at the end of the departure platform and 'an additional large gas lamp be placed at the head of the Second Class Refreshment Rooms'. Also

> that a transparent lamp be placed on the central line between the Leeds and Liverpool stations opposite the central window of the Refreshment Room on the interior platform with the words 'Refreshment Room' on the East and West sides, with plain glass towards the rails and towards the Refreshment Room.

Plate glass was fitted into the fan lights over two doors and lettered 'First and Second Class', and 'Third Class and Parcels Office'. To control public movement, it was ordered that 'entrance gates and lodges be erected and that they consist of a foot gate 6ft wide with a covered roof, then a lodge, then a carriage gate 12ft wide and the lodge and remaining space closed with iron pallisading'.[63]

From its opening on 1 January 1844, the new station was known as 'The Victoria Station', a much grander title than the Hunt's Bank Station which had been in use hitherto. Whether the Queen gave permission for the use of her name is open to discussion, but the following extract from a special meeting held on 28 December 1843 explains the derivation of the regal title. 'The Chairman said a proprietor had forwarded a proposition which he wished to be submitted to the meeting – that the designation of the new station in Manchester should be "The Victoria Station", as the Hunt's Bank Station did not appear to him to be appropriate'. In passing, the same edition of the *Manchester Guardian* noted that there began a half-hourly service of trains from Victoria Station to the station at Miles Platting (at first known as New Town Station), and that the stationary engines and the endless rope were not in operation, 'though quite perfect'. Moreover,

> The trains during the day are taken up the incline by two engines which drew twelve carriages with ease. Each train has with it a loaded small square waggon called a 'break waggon' which is provided with a break [sic] so powerful to be thereby enabled to stop the train at any part of the incline in case of accident.

As if to dispel any concern about the possibility of a train careering down the incline out of control, the news item concluded, 'Thus there is no accident that could take place, even the breaking of the endless chain [sic] or the failure of the stationary engine that could cause more than a few minutes delay'.

On 4 May 1844, the Liverpool & Manchester Company opened its extension line to Victoria Station, establishing at last the M&L Company's inveterate intention of forming an unbroken line of communication between Liverpool and Hull.

63. PRO RAIL 343/485

EIGHT

Running the M&L: 1839–1847

Few details exist which describe the locomotives, carriages and waggons used by the Company, along with the infrastructure which was established to build, repair and maintain them. The repair shops at Salford and Miles Platting, and the development of the engine sheds at the latter place remain largely enigmatic, rarely given any mention in the contemporary press or in official sources. Yet from the scanty information available it has been possible to gain some insight into how the MLR procured its motive power and rolling stock, and how it reacted to events which shaped the day-to-day operation of its services.

At the beginning of 1839 plans were made by the Company to establish a Locomotive Engine Department along with a supply of fuel for its engines. Committee of Management minutes are a valuable source of information and we can begin with those of 1 February 1839 where it was resolved,

1st, That the Committee recommends contracting with responsible and competent parties for the requisite supply of powers at a given price per passenger per mile and per ton of goods per mile or trip; if such responsible parties can be met with.

2nd, If competent parties cannot be contracted with . . . this Committee is of opinion that the next best plan will be for the Company to engage a first-rate Superintendent of the Locomotive Department.

3rd, If the Company be unable to make arrangements on the plans suggested . . . this Committee recommends that an engagement be made with some respectable

and competent parties already employed in making and repairing locomotive engines, to superintend the power department of this Company.

The first and third options were abandoned possibly owing to the unsatisfactory situation of placing the high responsibility in the hands of others. The second option was chosen, and to this end it was resolved on 1 April 1839 that Mr John Todd (of Birmingham) was to be appointed the Superintendent at a salary of £260 for the first year, £280 for the second year, and £300 for the third year, the contract being for a period of three years, 'together with a house rent free at the Station'. Which station this alluded to is not known, but as Oldham Road Station was the main one which existed at the time of Todd's appointment, this would seem to be the most likely. There was a proviso that John Todd could be discharged at any time should he be deemed unsatisfactory.

Todd began his new career on Monday, 22 April, and quickly felt the hot breath of the MLR Board down his neck. The latter had received a report about the poor state of two of the Company's locomotives, *Lancaster* and *Junction*; on 5 June it was decided, with regret, that the Board had to express its dissatisfaction with Todd's own appointment of an incompetent driver who had allowed the locomotives to fall into disrepair. Todd was keen to leave the Company's service by the close of July 1840. Having found it difficult to work under Captain Laws, the Superintendent of the Line, he requested to be placed under Gooch, but his request was passed over, the result being that Todd resigned.[64]

64. John Marshall, *The Lancashire and Yorkshire Railway*, Vol.2, p.198.

Applications were received by the Board from William Jenkins and James Fenton, the decision as to which one being left to Robert Gill, the Managing Director. In the event, Gill chose James Fenton who was appointed, like Todd, on a three-year contract, and at a starting salary of £200 per year, rising to £240 in the third year, the same proviso which had applied to Todd's contract being appended. Fenton quickly supplied the Board with an assessment of the condition of the Company's engine stock, and was still at his post in February 1843 when things began to go wrong. A minute, dated 14 February, drew attention 'to a defective engine in a goods train. The engine had not been examined thoroughly before steam was got up'. Both Fenton and John C. Craven, the locomotive foreman were reprimanded for neglect of duty.[65] Fenton, however, continued at his post, not resigning until 20 February 1845, his place then being taken by William Jenkins who had been waiting in the wings at the Manchester & Bolton Railway Works in Salford.

An early engine shed occupied a site in the fork of land formed between the junction of the Oldham Road line and the Hunt's Bank Incline. The Minutes of the Committee of Management, 14 March 1839, refer to a Mr Forsyth who 'laid on the table and explained to the Committee the proposed plans for the engine shed at the Manchester terminus'.[66] Evidently, the contractors, Bowden & Edwards did not satisfy the Committee of Management, which, in a report dated 6 June 1839,

> Ordered a letter to be written to Messrs Bowden & Edwards to the effect that Mr Gooch had reported the progress which they had made in building the Manchester engine shed to be very unsatisfactory, and the Committee requested that more active measures should be employed.[67]

The Committee's exhortations to the contractors had some effect for a further reference is made to the engine shed on 5 December the same year in which Bowden & Edwards were awaiting the arrival of the turntable and that the shed was 'otherwise nearly finished'.[68]

The shed was not fully completed, however, when the first five locomotives were delivered by the firm of Robert Stephenson & Co. of Newcastle. The stock of engines were delivered to the Manchester end of the line which was a sensible arrangement since this was the first section of the railway to be opened. The M&L Board ordered their locomotives from private manufacturers to begin with because the Company had no provision for building them. The first three Stephenson locomotives were transported from Tyneside to Rochdale, a note in the Committee of Management Minutes stating that it was ordered 'That the Secretary write to Mr Garbutt of Hull desiring that the Locomotive Engines from Newcastle

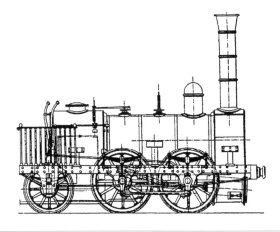

Robert Stephenson type 0-4-2 locomotive

TABLE B: Stephenson 0-4-2s built for the M&L

NO.	NAME	MAKER	DATE
1	*Stanley*	R. Stephenson & Co.	25 April 1839
2	*Kenyon*	ditto	28 April 1839
3	*Stephenson*	ditto	1 May 1839
4	*Lancaster*	Sharp Bros., Manchester	4 May 1839
5	*Junction*	ditto	18 May 1839
6	*York*	ditto	3 July 1839
7	*Rochdale*	Nasmyth & Co., Patricroft	16 July 1839
8	*Leeds* (?)	Shepherd & Todd, Leeds	?
9	*Bradford*	Nasmyth & Co.	6 Sept. 1839
10	*Hull*	ditto	7 Sept. 1839
11	*Scarborough*	Shepherd & Todd, Leeds	Sept. 1839
12	*Harrogate* (?)	ditto	?

65. Committee of Management Minutes, 14 February 1843.

66. PRO RAIL 343/485

67. Ibid.

68. Ibid.

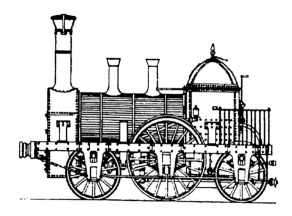

Robert Stephenson
type 2-2-2 locomotive

may be unshipped at Rochdale instead of Manchester[69], the inference being that part of the journey took advantage of the canal system between Yorkshire and Lancashire.

A reference to the locomotive *Scarborough* was made in *The Railway Times*, 28 September 1839, and provides a picture of how these heavy pieces of machinery were transported from factory to railway:

> A few days ago a new engine named 'The Scarborough' arrived from the manufactory of Messrs Shepherds [sic] & Todd of Leeds; it was a very fine engine loaded on a truck and required twenty horses to draw it; the wheels of the truck were frequently sunk into the ground and the exertion was very severe to get it to its destination. One of the horses was lamed, its leg being broken. The engine was forthwith placed upon the rails and would commence working when required.

Scarborough was one of the later engines, numbered 11 by the M&L, its approximate completion date being 9 September 1839.

Although the first three 0-4-2s were made by Robert Stephenson & Co., the same firm also supplied the Company with specifications and plans so that the same design could be manufactured by other firms of the Company's choice. TABLE B is a list of the 12 Stephenson 0-4-2s built for the M&L, and shows the maker's name together with the approximate date of completion/dispatch.[70]

Stanley was named after Lord Stanley, Chairman of the House of Commons Committee who supported the M&L Bill in 1836.

Other Stephenson designs followed: 19 engines, numbered 15 to 40, of the 2-2-2 wheel arrangement were delivered between October 1840 and April 1842. These were recommended by Stephenson to work the eastern section of the line, between Sowerby Bridge and Wakefield, thus gradually removing the M&L's reliance on North Midland Railway motive power which had at first prevailed from late in 1840. Once again several manufacturers were involved in the supply of these locomotives. Goods engines were represented by a further batch of 0-4-2s; 13 were delivered (nos 33 to 46)

TABLE C: Stephenson-designed 2-2-2 locomotives built for the M&L

NO.	NAME	MANUFACTURER	DATE BUILT OR DESPATCHED
15	Humber	Charles Tayleur & Co.	October 1840
16	Mersey	Charles Tayleur & Co.	October 1840
17	Aire	Rothwell & Co.	November 1840
18	Calder	Rothwell & Co.	November 1840
19	Dewsbury	Laird Kitson & Co.	December 1840
20	Towneley	Sharp Bros.	January 1841
21	Burnley	Sharp Bros.	January 1841
22	Derby	Nasmyth & Co.	18 January 1841
23	Sheffield	Nasmyth & Co.	22 January 1841
24	Trent	Rothwell & Co.	January 1841
25	Ouse	Rothwell & Co.	January 1841
26	Selby	Laird Kitson & Co.	January 1841
27	Irk*	W. Fairbairn & Co.	January 1841
28	Todmorden	Sharp Bros.	February 1841
29	Halifax	Sharp Bros.	February 1841
30	Manchester	Sharp Bros.	February 1841
31	Irwell	W. Fairbairn & Co.	February 1841
32	Wakefield	Sharp Bros.	March 1841
40	—	Laird Kitson& Co.	April 1842

* This engine exploded in Miles Platting engine shed on 28 January 1845 killing three men. Deodand of £500 was imposed on the engine, the Company complying with this without question.

69. PRO RAIL 343/485
70. Marshall, Vol.3, p.212.
71. Ibid.
72. PRO RAIL 343/845.
73. Ibid.
74. Ibid.
75. Ibid.

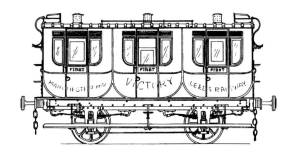
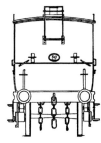

between April 1841 and June 1843, the three manufacturers involved being R. Stephenson & Co., Haigh Foundry, Wigan, and William Fairbairn & Co. of Manchester.

Three standard Bury-type 0-4-0s were the last engines to be delivered (nos 47 to 49) the first two bearing the names *West Riding Union* and *Cleckheaton* respectively. All three were completed between November 1845 and January 1846 by the firm of Edward Bury of Liverpool.[71]

There are various references to the acquisition of tools and equipment needed to maintain these locomotives. It was resolved on 1 April 1839 that because of the nearness of the Messrs Sharp Roberts & Co.'s works 'it appears to the Committee unnecessary to order any Spare Gear from them and that the names for three locomotive engines to be "Lancaster", "York", and "Junction"'.[72] On the other hand, where manufacturers were some distance away, it was resolved:

> That a set of Spare Gear be ordered for the Locomotive Engines – ordered from Messrs Robert Stephenson & Co., and that the Secretary address letters to the other parties from whom Locomotive Engines have been ordered requesting them to furnish a list of such parts as they consider should constitute the Spare Gear. [73]

Fuel also was an important consideration. The Minutes again provide a few details of how fuel for the engines could be obtained. Captain Laws, Superintendent of the Line, was authorised to negotiate the best terms he could for supplies of coke to the extent of 50 tons each. The suppliers were named as the Nordley Collieries, the Hulton Collieries, and the Clammerclough Collieries. On 2 May 1839, it was resolved:

> That Mr Hulton's offer to supply coal to the Company with coke be accepted to the extent of 100 tons per month at 25s per ton laid down at the station, and that the Company engage to give Mr Hulton three months notice should it be their wish at any time to terminate the Contract.[74]

Relations between the Company and the locomotive manufacturers and the suppliers of fuel were of major importance.

In the pioneering days it was essential to be on good terms with everyone. It worked the other way too. An example of early co-operation appeared in the Minutes dated 18 April 1839 when Messrs Sharp Roberts & Co. enquired whether the M&L Board 'had any objections to the Locomotive Engine "Lancaster" being tried on the Liverpool Railway'. The Board were happy to oblige, it being felt that it was

> very desirable that a trial of the Engine should take place and therefore that the permission asked by Messrs Sharp Roberts & Co. be granted and that they be also requested during the trial to ascertain the quality of the coke made from the Littleborough coals.[75]

Water too was a prerequisite for running locomotives. An investigation into the supplies of water was carried out and reported on by the Locomotive and Store Committee on 14 February 1843. It was calculated that water consumption

Above: First Class Coach, circa 1840. The guard's box seat was at roof level at each end. There were no brakes. Running boards allowed the guard/ticket collector to inspect tickets while the train was in motion!

Below: Second Class Coach, circa 1838 – a composite 'Gondola' carriage. The covered section was for First Class, leaving the open ends for Second Class passengers to enjoy the fresh air. This type of carriage had a short life

These drawings are based on limited information available and are intended to illustrate the type of carriages operated

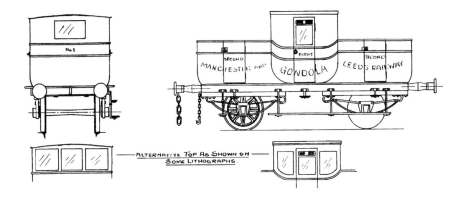

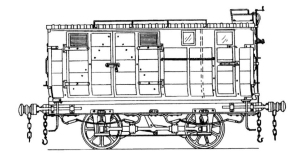

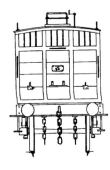

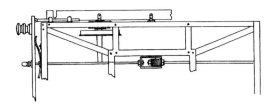

Above: Horse Van, circa 1840. Only two of these vehicles were built. The guard's seat at roof level enabled him to inspect the train while it was in motion. The roof-level brake handle operated primitive brake blocks which applied to each wheel

Below: Second Class Carriage, circa 1840. Thirty were built, numbered 20–49. With no partitions between compartments, seats were plain wood, and no lighting was provided. Windows could be closed with wooden slides

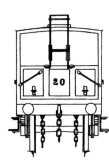

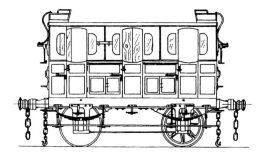

between Manchester and Leeds (via Normanton) would be 1,500 gallons for each engine; and that while passenger trains with their lighter loads could go from Manchester to Hebden Bridge without stopping for water, luggage trains 'must water at Rochdale'.

Rochdale was designated a 'reserved watering station' only to be used for water in cases of necessity. The consumption of water at Hebden Bridge was 18,000 gallons a day; this was pumped by hand and cost £90 per annum. Hebden Bridge was held to be 'a principal watering station, with two pumping gear operated by two men'. The cost of water at the Manchester station was £260 per annum; a suggestion was made that water could be delivered by pipes from Moston on the northern outskirts of the city. Like Rochdale, Sowerby Bridge and Dewsbury were designated reserved stations, while Brighouse paralleled Hebden Bridge. Wakefield town council supplied water at £180 per annum; to save money, Wakefield too would be a reserved station with the consumption of water 'reduced as much as possible'.[76]

A calamity befell the M&L on Tuesday, 20 January 1845, when, at 6 a.m, the boiler of the *Irk* engine (a Robert Stephenson 2-2-2) exploded inside the engine shed at Miles Platting. John Craven, the foreman, arrived at the scene shortly afterwards to find the shed partly in ruins, only the outer walls still standing. After a roll call, it was discovered that two men were missing; William Alcock, a fireman, and William Stone, a night watchman, were both killed. The engine was found upside down after being hurled through the roof of the shed, and landing in an inspection pit. The engine shed was described as a wooden building, 56 yards long, 21 yards of the roof of which was destroyed.[77] *Herapath*, reporting the incident a couple of weeks later, outlined details of the offending locomotive:

The Irk engine, No.27 of those belonging to the Company, was made by Messrs W. Fairbairn & Co., and was generally considered as one of the best on the line, doing its duty with less fuel than others. It was placed on the line in January 1841, in which month it ran 112 miles; and in the four years it had been at work it has run a aggregate distance of 76,860 miles.[78]

With an eye for detail, *Herapath* gave the weight of the engine, without tender, as 15½ tons in working order, and a cost of £1,430. On the day it exploded it was to have taken the 7.15 a.m. train from Manchester to Leeds.

In addition to the original round-house engine shed at Miles Platting, land to the rear of it was utilised for the M&L's own locomotive, carriage and waggon workshops. These were planned by John Hawkshaw, the Company's engineer, the construction of the buildings placed in the hands of David Bellhouse, the Manchester-based contractor. John Marshall tells us that Captain Laws informed the Board that the workshops had been completed by September 1845. He also informs us that the main building which comprised three floors,

was about 400 feet long and 75 feet wide. About three-quarters of the ground floor, to the north east, was for locomotives and the rest for carriages. The works stood at a lower level than the engine sheds and as built in 1846 the main building was temporarily approached by a steep incline from a siding beside the round-house'.[79]

The Minutes of the Locomotive and Carriage Committee, 1 February 1847, state that: 'Mr Hawkshaw proposes to erect the New Waggon Shop on the field purchased by the Company at Miles Platting opposite the present workshops'. Plans for this were accepted by the Board.[80]

Despite facilities for constructing their own locomotives and waggons, the same Committee Minutes indicate that outside contractors were still required to supply locomotives and rolling stock. For example, 'Mr Hawkshaw reported an offer from Bury Curtiss & Kennedy to supply the Company with 20 Engines and tenders, or upward, (according to pattern) at £2,300 each Engine and tender, to deliver 10 in 1848 and the rest in 1849'. The offer was accepted. The M&L workshops could not build carriages and waggons fast enough for requirements. A tender of Joseph Wright was accepted 'to construct 200 waggons to be delivered in 8 months . . . Also of Messrs Smith & Willie of Liverpool to supply the Company with 200 waggons at £77 per waggon'. Wright tendered for carriages and won the order according to the following specifications:

30 First Class @ £390 each.
20 Composite (First and Second Class) @ £345 each.
50 Second Class @ £290 each.
70 Third Class @ £220 each.

'Breaks [sic] to be £25 extra and to be applied to each of the Second and Third Class carriages, the whole to be delivered before 1 April 1848'.[81]

Tenders for carriages had been offered as early as 13 September 1838. The following item appeared in the Committee of Management Minutes:[82]

Mr Wm. Carr – First Class Carriage No.8 –
£400 for carriage; £25 for break.
Messrs Richard Melling & Co. – First Class Carriage
No.9 – £300 each carriage; £25 each break.

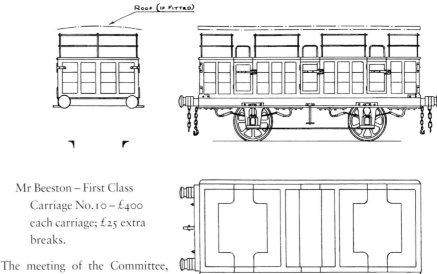

Mr Beeston – First Class Carriage No.10 – £400 each carriage; £25 extra breaks.

The meeting of the Committee, 24 September 1838, noted:

an order be given to Messrs Richard Melling & Co. for four First Class Carriages and the Breaks at £22 to be made according also to the specifications furnished by the Company and according also to supplemental specification now read over to Mr Melling and agreed to by him.

William Carr and H.H. Beeston also received orders for four carriages each, the latter having reduced his prices to £380 each carriage and £22 each brake, all to be delivered by 1 March 1839.[83]

At a further meeting on 27 October, the Secretary 'laid on the table two models of 3rd Class Carriages from Messrs Richard Melling & Co. whereupon the latter was requested to offer a tender and specification "according to Model No.1"'. The dimensions of this vehicle body was to be 6 ft 8 in., 'so as to allow a double seat, being placed in the centre of the carriage, and thereby rendered capable of containing 40 persons' [84] (!)

A fuller account of a typical M&L Third Class carriage appeared in the *Manchester Guardian* on 20 March 1839:

The other day we inspected a new railway carriage of what is usually called the third-class, having neither

Third Class Waggon, circa 1840. As originally built, the waggon had only one door on each side and there were no hand rails, seats, or brakes. The version shown here, however, is a modified one fitted with hand rails, wooden seating, and three doors on each side. Twenty such waggons were constructed. The lower view shows the internal seating arrangement

76. PRO RAIL 343/845.
77. *Manchester Guardian*, 29 January 1845.
78. *Herapath*, 1 February 1845.
79. Marshall, Vol.2, p.201.
80. PRO RAIL 343/519.
81. Ibid.
82. PRO RAIL 343/485.
83. Ibid.
84. Ibid

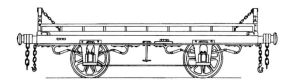

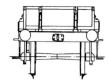

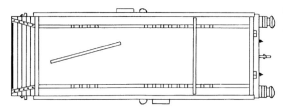

Carriage Waggon. The well-to-do could transport their private carriage by rail. To effect this carriage trucks were designed with ends which could be dropped down to enable a convenient roll-on/roll off facility at stations. Ten were built as early as 1838.

roof nor enclosed sides . . . It is 17 feet 10½ inches in length and 7 feet 11½ inches in width. The form of the carriage is not so square as hitherto used but more nearly resembling the form of a long boat with the stem and stern cut off and made square. A bench seat extends the whole length of the carriage on each side, and down the middle is another broad bench, 27½ inches in width dividing in the middle by an open rail or back of wood rising to a height of 14 inches from the seat, so as to form two benches on which passengers sit back-to-back. Allowing 14 inches to each passenger, the carriage would seat about 60 persons. Ascent is had by two broad iron footplates at each corner of the carriage so that there are four doors affording ready ingress and egress. An iron rail extends along the sides of the carriage so as to prevent anything from falling over. The exterior of the carriage is painted olive green and is formed into panels. The whole is a neat appearance and is capable of accommodating a great number of passengers than any other carriage we have seen of equal dimensions.

Travelling in such a vehicle, especially when crowded with people of different shapes and sizes, not to mention unappealing attributes, must have been a miserable experience over a distance of up to five miles or more. The wonders of this carriage may be compared with that of a First Class carriage described in *The Railway Times*, 20 March 1841:

A carriage for the Leeds Railway has just been

completed from the designs by the Chief Superintendent, Captain Laws RN, and built by Messrs Melling & Son [sic], coach builders, Greenheys; which for beauty and workmanship, together with utility and convenience, may be considered almost unequalled. The body is 18 feet long by 7 feet wide and built after the Italian gondolas, with a centre compartment 8 feet long by 7 feet wide, and 6 feet 6 inches high; allowing parties to promenade with the head covered. The interior of this compartment is fitted up to give the appearance of a splendid saloon with rich carved mahogany sofas lined with crimson plush and trimmed with silk gymp, and at each corner is a mirror of large dimensions. The painting is of very superior character, the body being of a handsome lemon colour; and above the panels are emblazoned the arms of Manchester, Leeds, London, York, Hull, Birmingham, and Derby, painted in most beautiful relief to the rich and delicate body colour. The lightness of the undercarriage is equally characteristic with the superior accommodation of the interior. The buffing apparatus consists of a box of small elliptic springs with single plates, each corner being free from those large and heavy buffer springs hitherto used.

Opulence indeed for those who were fortunate enough to appreciate it.

The M&L had, by an Act of 18 July 1846, absorbed the Manchester & Bolton Railway and thereby that Company's locomotive and rolling stock. A return[85] of the rolling stock appeared in the Locomotive and Carriage Committee Minutes, dated 4 November 1846, a few months after the take-over, the actual transfer being made on paper on 24 September of that year. The stock consisted of:

12 locomotives; 15 First Class carriages; 22 Second Class carriages; 14 Third Class carriages; 2 smoking carriages (First and Second Class); 4 horse boxes, 4 carriage trucks; 2 parcel vans for passenger trains; and three parcel vans for delivery of parcels.

85. PRO RAIL 343/519.

86. *The Railway Record*, 7 March 1846.

87. PRO RAIL 343/519.

Several items of rolling stock were in the course of delivery when the MLR take-over occurred, namely:

10 coupé carriages (First and Second Class);
6 Second Class; 10 Third Class; 1 parcel van.

Whilst in the waggon list the following were also due for delivery:

100 coal waggons; 88 luggage waggons; 10 cattle waggons; 9 coke waggons; 6 passenger waggons (Third Class); 6 ballast waggons; 2 stone lorries; and 6 road men's lorries.

Before the Manchester, Bolton & Bury was absorbed, this Company's locomotives and rolling stock were repaired and maintained at their Salford works, the latter becoming part of the MLR western section under the supervision of William Hurst after the take-over on 18 July 1846.

At a half-yearly meeting on 4 March 1846 it was stated that 'much difficulty was experienced throughout the year in procuring an adequate supply of carriages, waggons, and engines, to meet the rapid increase in traffic'.[86] The take-over of the Manchester & Bolton company must have heartened the Locomotive Superintendent, William Jenkins, whose stock of locomotives stood at 49 before the acquisition of the Bolton company.

In order to reach York and Hull, it was necessary for the M&L to run its trains over York & North Midland metals from Altofts, Normanton. On such occasions, both companies' carriages were mixed in trains going on from Normanton. According to Y&NM Board Minutes of 20 February 1847, complaints were constantly made by passengers riding in the M&L vehicles 'of the very unsteady motion of the carriages'. The violent oscillation experienced was alleged to have been caused by the imperfect method of coupling used on the M&L stock. The Y&NM made a formal complaint to the M&L Directors and called for 'a remedy to the problem'. In turn, the M&L informed the Y&NM that it was substituting the screw coupling as 'fast as possible'.[87]

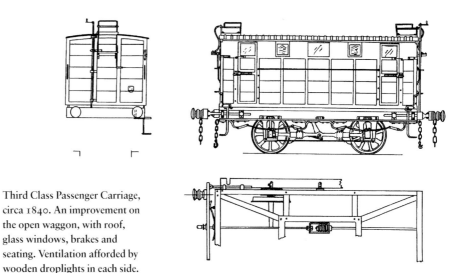

Third Class Passenger Carriage, circa 1840. An improvement on the open waggon, with roof, glass windows, brakes and seating. Ventilation afforded by wooden droplights in each side. No lighting

One facility the M&L never possessed were water troughs! Located in a cutting between Luddenden Foot and Sowerby Bridge, were these troughs 502 yds long, laid by the LYR between 1885 and 1890. Here we see LMS NO.10885 on a Leeds-Bradford-Manchester stopping train in 1937, a little over one hundred years to the year when the M&L was formed. Photo Gordon Coltas

NINE

The Bronte Connection

MUCH has been written about Branwell Bronte and his connection with the M&L Railway – there are two literary works both devoted to the brother of the three well-known sisters; namely Daphne du Maurier's *The Infernal World of Branwell Bronte* (1960) and Winifred Gerin's *Branwell Bronte* (1961). A more recent book (1994) has thrown fresh light on the Brontes, with newly-researched material alluding specifically to Branwell during his time with the Company. It is from Juliet Barker's scholarly work *The Brontes* that the following account is gratefully drawn.

Some facts are unassailable; Branwell was born on 26 June 1817, the only son of the Reverend Patrick and Maria Bronte. They lived at Thornton, about four miles out of Bradford, and it was at the Old Bell Chapel in Thornton that the infant was baptized Patrick Branwell on the 23 July. The question arises as to why, at 22, he ever contemplated a career on the railways, since it seems remote from his upbringing within a religious and ecclesiastical ambience. Perhaps this can be explained by the fact that Branwell had been thwarted in his aspirations to enter the world of writing and painting, and although this craving to create by way of prose, poetry and painting was to stay with him, opportunities to emulate his sisters were to elude him. Branwell's wish to enter the Royal Academy of Art at 18 had not materialised – his written work, however, found a place in *Blackwood's Magazine*.

In the summer of 1840, Branwell decided to find work on the railway then in the final stages of construction between Hebden Bridge and Normanton. The nearest point of the line to the family home in Haworth was between Hebden Bridge and Sowerby Bridge. It was to be a meeting of two different worlds: a man with literary and artistic ambitions coming face-to-face with the industry of rough men, machinery and steam. It was, however, a world which had fascinated him:

> Branwell had apparently been taking a great deal of interest in the construction of the railway and leapt at the opportunity to work on it. It may seem strange today that anyone should have found the prospect of working on the railways exciting, but it is forgotten what an immense and pioneering project it was.[88]

Branwell's appointment was confirmed at a Board Meeting held at Hunt's Bank on 31 August 1840, the post of 'assistant clerk-in-charge' to be taken at the newly-opened station at Sowerby Bridge, at an annual salary of £75, rising by £10 a year to a maximum of £105. This was a relatively low salary and much less than Branwell could have received as a private tutor, although the prospects of promotion were far better. The clerk-in-charge at Sowerby Bridge, George Duncan, in contrast, had been engaged on a salary of £130, this too increasing by increments to a maximum of £150.

On 5 October 1840, Sowerby Bridge Station was bedecked with bunting and flags, and thronged with onlookers who hoped to see the first train pass through. Branwell was there too manning his post as an officer of the Company. The days following this event became more routine. Only three trains ran each way through the station until the opening of the

Self portrait of Branwell Bronte in pencil, *c.*1840

88. Juliet Barker, *The Brontes*, Phoenix, 1995, p.345.

Summit Tunnel which had the immediate effect of increasing the traffic eightfold. Now there was much to do: 'The clerk and his assistant were therefore kept busy logging the trains and their cargoes, organising and co-ordinating the loading and unloading of waggons, and supervising the safety of passengers'.[89] Branwell is supposed to have lodged at the Pear Tree Inn at Sowerby Bridge, overlooking the railway, but this has been refuted. It is more likely that instead of a beer house, he found more gentlemanly lodgings in a suite of rooms with a respectable family. Sowerby Bridge in 1841 was an industrial centre of about 5,000 people, many employed in the town's cotton, woollen, worsted, and corn mills which were located in the valley bottom often adjacent to the canals. Ancillary industry had also developed in the form of the gas works, chemical works, and iron foundries.

Promotion for Branwell came on 1 April 1841 when he was transferred to Luddenden Foot Station as clerk-in-charge at an improved salary of £130 a year. Here Branwell made his acquaintance with Francis Grundy, a young railway engineer who painted a grim picture of Branwell's workplace:

> When I first met him [Branwell], he was station
> master at a small roadside place on the Manchester
> and Leeds Railway, Luddenden Foot by name. The
> line was only just opened. This station was a rude
> wooden hut, and there was no village near at hand.[90]

Luddenden Foot was a tiny centre of the woollen trade which existed both a cottage industry and in the new stone-built mills. Grundy maintained that Branwell was cut off from his literary and artistic friends, hence his unsettled frame of mind at this time, but as a railway employee, he would have been able to travel free-of-charge by train, and could reach Hebden Bridge and Sowerby Bridge within five minutes, whilst Manchester and Leeds were less than two hours away. Nevertheless, it is accepted wisdom that Branwell's time at Luddenden Foot was the start of his journey on the road to ruin. 'Branwell spent his time in the pubs of the Calder Valley, neglected his job, doodled in the margins of the company ledgers, and, as Grundy would have it, went thoroughly to the bad'.[91]

In March 1842 a Company audit of the ledgers at Luddenden Foot Station was undertaken. An eagle-eyed auditor spotted a discrepancy in the figures to the tune of £11 1s 7d, which Branwell could not account for. Although held responsible, he was not charged with fraud or theft, but according to Grundy, 'convicted of constant and culpable carelessness'. The sum was deducted from his salary and his dismissal took effect from the Board of Directors meeting on 4 March 1842.

Was Branwell's offence so serious as to warrant his dismissal? Had he been accused of theft or fraudulent fixing of the figures, the dismissal would have been accompanied by prosecution and imprisonment. The M&L Railway Company followed to the letter Lord Seymour's Act as was evidenced by the number of relatively contemporaneous incidents which had incurred harsh penalties. The *Halifax Guardian* reported these on different occasions: 16 January 1841 – three men prosecuted for taking two cranes along the line without displaying lights or signals thereby causing a crash at Sowerby Bridge. 27 March 1841 – Joseph Cobden, discharged and prosecuted for derailing a train at Brighouse because he forgot to change the points. 4 December 1841 – Four men arrested for causing a crash at Luddenden Foot when they travelled along the line on a truck after a drinking bout, and ran into a train, which caused serious injuries to two of them.

Drunkenness was regarded as a most serious offence and had Branwell, who had a penchant for drink, been found drunk and in dereliction of duty, the penalty imposed would have been a term in prison with hard labour. However, this was not the case and those around who knew him, local merchants and manufacturers, and friends, set up a petition to be presented to the Board, but without success. Although humiliated and disgraced, Branwell waited for two months before seeking Francis Grundy's support in obtaining a new post with the Company – but it was not to be, the Company unmoved by his plea for a second chance. This marked the end of the Bronte connection with the M&L Railway, Branwell eventually dying from a *mélange* of drink, opium and tuberculosis on 24 September 1848, after a desultory life and with his ambitions unfulfilled.

89. Juliet Barker, *The Brontes*, Phoenix, 1995, p.346.

90. Ibid, p.367.

91. Ibid, p.367.

TEN

Thomas Edmondson and the Defeat of Fraud

During the first public day of the railway traffic, Thursday last, there were, as might be expected, many attempts at imposition, almost altogether by individuals going in third-class carriages.

So lamented the *Manchester Guardian* in its edition of 8 July 1839, sadly reflecting the human propensity to cheat and defraud whenever an advantage could be gained, in this case, over a fledgling enterprise, the Manchester & Leeds Railway. Swindling the Company was a relatively easy activity. As newly-established public amenities the railways had to find their feet, instruct novice staff, as well as organise the throngs of individuals who pressed for a ticket to take the train on their first, second, or tenth ride. A large part of the problem of fraud lay in the outdated method of booking passengers at stations, a method which was based on stage-coach practice. 'In the first days of railway travelling it was natural that the kind of tickets which had served for coach passengers should still be used as vouchers that a traveller had paid his fare'.[92] The voucher was handed to the guard who had enough to do without the extra responsibility of trying to remember where each passenger was travelling to. The same system, naturally adopted by the first railways,

Thomas Edmondson from a drawing by Sheila Pamphilon, of unknown date

was cumbersome and wide open to the abuse of anyone determined enough to obtain a free ride, or travel further than the fare permitted. Ticketing varied according to a particular company's ideas on the matter – it was always a case of trial and error. Take, for instance, the method employed on the Liverpool & Manchester Railway:

On such new ground, the Directors made a meal of it; each passenger had to give twenty-four hours notice, and supply name, address, age, place of birth, occupation and reason for travelling: more of a passport than a railway ticket. For each train, a waybill containing the names of all the passengers was handed to the guard.[93]

The M&L Railway, despite the experiences of its neighbouring company, also incurred problems owing to the want of a better, more fool-proof system. Some travellers quickly learned that they could outwit the railway by such devious means as travelling without a ticket, and hiding under the seat or a blanket, and buying a ticket the price of which fell short of the journey they intended to make. The Company's only recourse, after obtaining the correct fare, was to placard offenders at their railway stations as well as to take the matter to court where a

92. *English Mechanic and World of Science Journal*, No.697, 2 August 1878.

93. Frank Ferneyhough, *Liverpool & Manchester Railway 1830–1980*, p.105.

fine was levied. The way was open, however, for someone to devise a system by which all but the most ruthless could be deterred and prevented from fraudulant travel.

In 1836 Thomas Edmondson became known as 'the originator or inventor of the ticket system, which is now adopted by almost every railway company throughout the land'.[94] Born at Lancaster on 30 June 1792, the son of John and Jane Edmondson, he was one of a family of twelve siblings. His parents 'were of humble and respectable extraction, and educated their children to the best of their ability, giving to each that share which his or her talent seemed to warrant, and inclination as to literary or mechanical pursuits seemed to require'.[95] Edmondson, from an early age, displayed an inventive trait: one of his earliest inventions was described as 'One piece of mechanism . . . by which the busy housewife was able to churn the butter and rock the cradle at the same time'.[96]

Both as an apprentice cabinet maker, and afterwards as a journeyman furniture maker with the firm of Waring and Co., of Lancaster, Edmondson gained the skills in woodworking which placed him in good stead in the future. An unsuccessful partnership in a cabinet-making business at Carlisle led to bankruptcy, and yet, despite debts, he still endeavoured to pay off his creditors. Edmondson then spent a short time in the tea and grocery business, a time which confirmed that he was not best suited to the world of running a business. The Newcastle & Carlisle Railway opened its line between Carlisle and Greenhead on 19 July 1836. Stimulated by this occasion, Edmondson turned his attention to the railways (echoes of Branwell Bronte) as a source of income, and successfully applied, against a number of competitors, for the post of station master-cum-booking clerk at the remote wayside Milton Station, 14 miles east of Carlisle. It was while in this position that he realised the need for a method of issuing tickets which would facilitate booking passengers more expeditiously and at the same time eliminate fraud. From his firsthand experience as booking clerk, he took the matter one step further in finding 'that little or no systematic check was imposed upon the station clerks, it being left to their integrity to account correctly for monies paid to them'.[97] Thus not only was a check to be made on the travelling public but also on those who issued the tickets and handled the money in the first place.

During his employment at Milton Station, the first steps were taken by Edmondson to improve the ticketing system. Using his own cabinet-making tools and workbench, a number of devices were made so that details could be printed on to a strip of cardboard which was then cut by scissors into tickets. A ticket-dispensing cabinet was also made along with the introduction of a numbering system which gave at a glance a means of counting the number of tickets sold. The Newcastle Company, in full knowledge of this innovation at Milton, chose to ignore it, although it was probably recognised that in Edmondson, the Company had more than a mere booking clerk: 'There was a proposition to remove him to Newcastle, but it was not carried into effect, and the repeated delays were very disheartening to him'.[98] This moment of Company indecision enabled the M&L's Captain Laws who, having learned of the innovation, decided to visit Milton to have the details explained to him thoroughly. It was the clear-sighted Laws who saw the potential of the Edmondson system, one in which the M&L could adopt to its own advantage, and to the benefit of other railways. Captain Laws was evidently much impressed: 'He therefore proposed at once to Mr Edmondson that he should

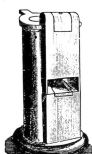

ORIGINAL RIBBON PRESS.
(ORIGINAL PATTERN PRESS).

TYPE BOX WITH TYPE SUPPLIED
WITH EACH PRESS.

An Edmondson ticket printing and numbering press of 1845

Left: Ticket dating presses

94. *English Mechanic and World of Science Journal*, No.697, 2 August 1878.

95. Ibid.

96. Ibid.

97. Ibid.

98. Ibid.

remove to Manchester, with the object of introducing his system on the above railway, making the promise "that his salary be multiplied by two", an offer which, after due consideration, was gratefully accepted'.[99] At a Committee of Management meeting, 28 March 1839, it was resolved that 'Mr Thomas Edmondson be appointed a first-class Clerk or auditor in the Passenger Department at a salary of £200 per annum; and that he provide satisfactory security to the amount of £400'.[100]

Thus Edmondson left the bucolic charm of Milton to become the chief booking clerk at the Oldham Road Station, Manchester, in May 1839, and was given a free rein to introduce his invention throughout the M&L Railway. The *Manchester Guardian*, 8 July 1839, examined the procedure as adopted in readiness for the partial opening between Manchester and Littleborough:

The tickets are small, stiff cards, each having printed on its face the place of the passenger's destination, and an intimation that the passenger is to show the ticket to the Company's servants if required. Each ticket also bears at one end some small embossed figures which constitute its progressive number. The face of each ticket is white; and on one end is legibly stamped the date of issue. The back of the ticket is a different colour for each station.

The system of colour-coding on the reverse side of the ticket enabled the guard/ticket collector to see at a glance to which station the ticket allowed the passenger to travel: Mills Hill, blue; Rochdale, green; Littleborough, yellow. In addition, tickets for journeys from Manchester had the emblem of a fleece engraved on the back of the ticket whilst tickets for trains to Manchester displayed a cotton bale or bag. Yet a further embellishment was to indicate the class of conveyance the passenger was entitled to be in:

those for the first-class carriages have plain backs ... (except for the colour and the emblem) the second-class tickets have several horizontal lines drawn along the back; and those of the third-class have the back divided by perpendicular and horizontal lines into small squares, or what might be called a check pattern.[101]

This sophisticated system was first utilised on the day of the partial opening of the line between Manchester and Littleborough, and by its use, 110 attempts at fraudulent travel were detected. On the following day, further attempts to cheat the Company were again foiled:

At Rochdale, for instance, an individual taking a third-class ticket to Littleborough (6d) attempted to come to Manchester, but, in a few minutes after the

A ticket printing machine invented by Edmondson

Right: Railway-ticket issuing case invented by Thomas Edmondson

99. *English Mechanic and World of Science Journal*, No.697, 2 August 1878.

100. PRO RAIL 343/485.

101. *Manchester Guardian*, 8 July 1839.

Fronts of tickets

train had started, the guard, by means of the long footboards to the carriages, which enables him to walk along and collect tickets while the train is in motion, commenced collecting the tickets, and finding a yellow one amongst those which ought only to be either blue or pink, the passenger was told that he had got into the wrong train. He persisted that he had paid to Manchester; but, of course, he could not, in that case, have received a yellow ticket.[102]

The offender, on this occasion, was given the option of either to pay the full fare, or to alight at Mills Hill, 6d being the fare from Rochdale to that station.

The Edmondson system was a boon to the M&L Railway. As the number of passengers increased so the need for an expeditious way of handling tickets took on a new meaning. *Herapath*, 24 August 1839, tells us something about how operations were conducted at the Company's railway stations:

The business on this railway continues very rapidly to increase . . . the number of passengers conveyed on Monday having been no fewer than 4,365, while yesterday, they reached 4,704; total for the two days, 9,069. We are happy to state that Mr Edmondson's system of issuing tickets has fully met the pressure of business . . . On Monday, 1,519 passengers were booked at the Rochdale station with equal ease and despatch.

While carrying out his duties at Oldham Road Station, Edmondson continued to modify and perfect his invention, calling upon his various contacts in Carlisle and Lancaster to furnish metal components. John Blaylock, a Carlisle bell-founder, supplied the iron castings for dating presses which could be supplied to each station as it opened. A guillotine was manufactured whereby the strips of card could be cut out to the correct size, that is 2¼ in. by 1¼ in. The opening of the line throughout on 1 March 1841 brought with it a decision to display the number of each station on the ticket instead of using a colour-code. A further change appeared in that passengers now surrendered their tickets to the collector at the stations on completion of their journeys. This was probably a wise measure since the inspection of tickets by the guard while the train was moving was fraught with danger. This method of inspecting tickets, however, appeared to continue despite the concern expressed by the Board of Trade. *The Railway Times*, 17 October 1840, reported a serious accident

102. *Manchester Guardian*, 8 July 1839.

Back of a ticket to Brighouse

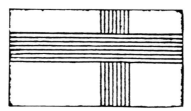

Back of a ticket to Eastwood

Back of a ticket to Horbury

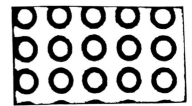

Back of a ticket to Hebden Bridge

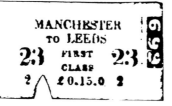

Fronts of tickets

JOHN B. EDMONDSON, MANCHESTER,

RAILWAY TICKET NIPPERS.

SPECIMEN OF VARIOUS CUTS MADE BY NIPPERS.

NO. 1   2   3   4   5   6   7   8   9   10   11

NO. 12   13   14   15   16   17   20   21   23   24   25

NO. 26   27   28   29   30   31   33

The Ticket Nipper is chiefly used to show that the railway ticket has passed examination at a certain station, or to cancel the ticket altogether.

I make a special Railway Ticket Nipper, with moveable type, to indent the current date into the ticket, each being supplied with a type to cut a private mark, used by inspectors.

PRICES ON APPLICATION.

The Nipper system was proposed in 1848 for dating by cut-outs rather than by an inked date. The proposal was to have 31 different shapes to distinguish different days of the month, the first 12 also being used for the months. There is no evidence that the system was ever adopted

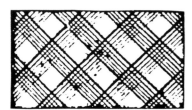

Back of a ticket to Wakefield

Back of a ticket to non-M&L destinations

on a Manchester-bound train, where the guard 'employed in the highly reprehensible and dangerous practice of collecting passengers' tickets by striding along the footboards from one carriage to another while the train was in motion', was badly injured by missing his foothold.

Despite the success with which the Edmondson system had been employed, the incidence of attempted fraudulent travel continued. For example, *Herapath*, 28 March 1840, reported that,

> On Thursday, two persons came down the line without paying the regular fare and obtaining tickets accordingly, expecting that they would have been able to elude the vigilance of the guards, but being detected, they were taken into custody and subsequently taken before the Borough Court . . . The magistrates gave the full penalty, 40s and costs, but it was commuted to 10s penalty, in order to carry one week's imprisonment.

In the summer of 1841, Edmondson resigned from the M&L: 'that Company, with a complimentary minute of the board, liberated him from their service, in order that he might devote his whole time to the further development and introduction of his system'.[103] Despite his early experiences, he set up his own business, severing his connection with the M&L. The *English Mechanic and World of Science Journal*, 2 August 1878, completed its eulogy of the 'ticket' man with:

> Little did he think at the lonely Milton station as he worked at his bench in the still hours of the night, of the ultimate extent and success with which his labours were to be crowned . . . At the close of a period of infirmity, extending over a year or two, and arising from overtaxed energies, he died at his residence in Manchester after a short illness on the 22nd June 1851, having nearly completed his 59th year.

103. *English Mechanic and World of Science Journal*, No.697, 2 August 1878.

ELEVEN

The End of an Era:
The Advent of another

The extended district now embraced by the lines belonging to the Company suggested the propriety of adopting a title more expressive of the extent and importance of the united system than that of the parent Company; and your Directors suggest that the future title of the Company be THE LANCASHIRE AND YORKSHIRE RAILWAY.

Henry Houldsworth – Chairman

THESE words were spoken at the 21st half-yearly meeting of shareholders of the Manchester & Leeds Company, held on 10 March 1847, at the Palatine Hotel, Manchester. The assembly was 'an unusually large one'; perhaps the knowledge that this marked the last half-yearly meeting of what the Chairman had termed 'the parent Company' had an added attraction, and the anticipation that a new railway era was about to commence drew in more than the usual number of interested parties. At the meeting, Henry Houldsworth intimated that the Directors had been approached by 'some proprietor in the room' suggesting that the title of the Company should be 'The Lancashire and Yorkshire Union Railways', and this might have been but for the desire of the Directors to keep the name 'as short as possible'.[104]

A decision to change the name had been taken earlier on 9 December 1846, and it was not until 9 July the following year that the change was ratified by an Act of Parliament.[105]

What was the background to this change of identity? On 21 March 1846, *The Times* issued an article in which the M&L Company was mildly rebuked for its undesirable aggressive policy of amalgamation. The Company's circuitous sixty-mile main line route had been rigorously defended by the Company against opponents to the original scheme and to subsequent competitors. This the Directors had done by 'buying up existing competitors and extending their influence in every quarter . . . to protect the parent line'.[106] Step by step, the M&L had attempted to remove its competition either by absorbing existing companies, promoting new lines of its own into virgin territory, and by co-operating with other companies in jointly-leased schemes. *The Times* article spelt out clearly a catalogue of take-overs in Yorkshire, and then turned its attention to Lancashire where similar overtures had been made to such disparate companies as the Manchester, Bolton & Bury Railway (absorbed on 15 July 1846) and the Preston & Wyre Railway (absorbed on 18 July the same year). *The Times* envisaged an eventual take-over of the East Lancashire Railway and its connections with other companies, thereby blocking

This polished granite tablet adorns an exterior wall of Littleborough Station and reminds everyone approaching of the origins of the building

104. *The Railway Record*, 13 March 1847.

105. John Marshall, *The Lancashire & Yorkshire Railway*, Vol.1, p.65.

106. *The Times*, 21 March 1846.

Aspinall 4-4-0 No.1103 and 4-4-2 No.1421 haul a Leeds-bound Dining Car Express through Middleton Junction in the final years of the LYR period. Both locomotives were withdrawn by 1929. It was at Middleton Junction that the line to Oldham, and the branch to Middleton left the main line. When the M&L reached this point the local area was known as Kay Lane End, a backwater betwixt Middleton and Chadderton. Author

107. *The Times*, 21 March 1846.

108. Jack Simmons, *The Railways of Britain*, p.13.

an alternative route between Liverpool and Leeds. This, however, did not materialise, the ELR remaining stoutly independent until its amalgamation with the L&Y on 13 May 1859. Observing the increase in such amalgamations, *The Times* considered that 'It requires no stretch of imagination to contemplate the possibility (unless Parliament sooner steps in) of amalgamation by which the whole kingdom will be under tribute to a gigantic monopoly'.[107]

Herein lay the source of *The Times*' anxiety: that railway monopolies were an unhealthy development, and far from the milieu of *laissez-faire* and free competition. Yet, as Jack Simmons has pointed out, the growth of the M&L was but an example of end-one amalgamation 'a type of union that was never open to the charge of attempting to set up a monopoly'.[108] Nevertheless, by dint of its policy of expansion, the M&L Company, and the incipient L&Y Company, survived all attempts to prevent the spread of its influence throughout Lancashire and Yorkshire. It was, in fact, unstoppable, except for the Company's failure to secure the purchase of the

Rochdale Canal Company. Under the chairmanship of Henry Houldsworth, the L&Y Company looked ahead with confidence, just as the M&L directors had in 1837 at its inception. John Hawkshaw had now assumed the mantle of Chief Engineer and his report at the first L&Y meeting (or what would have been the 22nd half-yearly meeting of the M&L) on 1 September 1847, gave a precise outline of the work in hand. His report ranged over the following: The Ashton Branch; the Oldham Mumps Extension; the Heywood Branch and its extension to Bury; the Burnley Branch; the Ardwick Branch; the Wakefield, Pontefract & Goole Railway; the Askern and Methley branches; the Liverpool & Bury Railway; the Huddersfield & Sheffield Railway; the West Riding Union Railway; the Bacup Branch; the Middleton Branch; the Horbury Bridge Branch and Whitley Branch.

All these reveal the wide-ranging ambit of influence sustained by the Company in the autumn of 1847; in short, these were the principal real concerns of the Directors of the Lancashire & Yorkshire Railway.

INDEX